SHAKESPEARE BEYOND SCIENCE:

WHEN POETRY WAS THE WORLD

ESSENTIAL ESSAYS SERIES 74

**Canada Council
for the Arts**

**Conseil des Arts
du Canada**

**ONTARIO ARTS COUNCIL
CONSEIL DES ARTS DE L'ONTARIO**

an Ontario government agency
un organisme du gouvernement de l'Ont

Canada

Guernica Editions Inc. acknowledges the support of the Canada Council
for the Arts and the Ontario Arts Council. The Ontario Arts Council
is an agency of the Government of Ontario.

We acknowledge the financial support of the Government of Canada.

SKY GILBERT

SHAKESPEARE BEYOND SCIENCE:
WHEN POETRY WAS THE WORLD

GUERNICA
EDITIONS

TORONTO – CHICAGO – BUFFALO – LANCASTER (U.K.)
2020

Michael Mirolla, editor
Cover and interior design: Errol F. Richardson
Cover image: Nicholas Hilliard's miniature:
Man Grasping a Hand from a Cloud
Guernica Editions Inc.
287 Templemead Drive, Hamilton (ON), Canada L8W 2W4
2250 Military Road, Tonawanda, N.Y. 14150-6000 U.S.A.
www.guernicaeditions.com

Distributors:
Independent Publishers Group (IPG)
600 North Pulaski Road, Chicago IL 60624
University of Toronto Press Distribution,
5201 Dufferin Street, Toronto (ON), Canada M3H 5T8
Gazelle Book Services, White Cross Mills
High Town, Lancaster LA1 4XS U.K.

First edition.
Printed in Canada.

Legal Deposit – Third Quarter
Library of Congress Catalog Card Number: 2019949191
Library and Archives Canada Cataloguing in Publication
Title: Shakespeare beyond science : when poetry was the world / Sky Gilbert.
Names: Gilbert, Sky, 1952- author.
Series: Essential essays series ; 74.
Description: Series statement: Essential essays series ; 74
Identifiers: Canadiana (print) 20190177306 | Canadiana (ebook) 20190177349 | ISBN
9781771835039   (softcover) | ISBN 9781771835046 (EPUB) | ISBN 9781771835053 (Kindle)
Subjects: LCSH: Shakespeare, William, 1564-1616—Knowledge and learning. | LCSH: Shakespeare,
William, 1564-1616—Philosophy. | LCSH: Shakespeare, William, 1564-1616—Language. |
LCSH:
Shakespeare, William, 1564-1616—Knowledge—Science.
Classification: LCC PR3001 .G55 2020 | DDC 822.3/3—dc23

*Dedicated to Lynne Kositsky and Roger Stritmatter:
for their impeccable scholarship and inspiration*

Our true intent is all for your delight,
We are not here that you should repent you.
The actors are at hand, and by their show,
You shall know all that you are like to know.
  —*A Midsummer Night's Dream* 5.1. (punctuation; mine)

The work of art does not aim to convey something else, just
itself.
  —**Wittgenstein**

Contents

Shakespeare the Rhetorician

Why does Shakespeare fascinate? One might argue that there are far too many books on this subject already. In fact why study Shakespeare at all? Certainly Shakespeare supports a booming cottage industry – quite literally – as the Shakespeare Birthplace Trust trots about daily, escorting eager tourists to cottages in Stratford where Shakespeare is said to have been born. As devil's advocate I remember that lone voice (but he spoke for so many of us!) in my high school English class, who – after a particularly complex and taxing analysis of a difficult passage from "the bard" (we didn't have "No Fear Shakespeare" back then) – whined: "If that's what he meant, why didn't the guy just come out and say it?" This is more than just the howl of a philistine; it cuts to the very essence of what makes Shakespeare relevant as we approach the quarter mark of the 21st century.

The secret lies in Shakespeare's language – not in the characters, the moral ideas or the "meaning." My approach to Shakespeare is not a popular one. Not because we are too stupid to grasp it, but because it is related to an antique and significantly alien manner of perceiving the world. In the late 1500's in England western culture was experiencing a monumental paradigm shift. Shakespeare was at the very centre of it, and – contrary to what you might imagine – he was, to some degree, a soldier in the old, medieval guard. So a true understanding of Shakespeare – that is, if we allow ourselves to be bewitched in the manner that he meant to bewitch us – will literally deliver us to another world.

This is not to suggest that Shakespeare delivers us backward in time – although, technically speaking, his work much more resembles medieval writing than it does modern writing. But ultimately, a true understanding of Shakespeare will take us forward. (Please note that for reasons that will become clear I hesitate to say it will *improve* us.) Of course if you have a teleological and optimistic view of human history you may not agree with an assertion that a confirmed "medievalist" like Shakespeare has much to offer us today. But my view of history is more cyclical. At any rate there is nothing more valuable than being able to step out of the box that we are in, and gaze at the world in a different way.

A warning. This book contains a critique of science – and I would argue that science is the driving force behind modern western thought. Mathematics and geometry are ancient, but what we call science today – that is, the scientific method that tests truth, partnered with the logic to argue for that truth – was effectively *discovered* by Francis Bacon, during Shakespeare's lifetime. I am not anti-technology, or anti-science. But science is arguably our new philosophy, our new religion, and to quote Hamlet: "There are more things in heaven and earth Horatio, than are dreamt of in your philosophy."[1] Here I do not make the common mistake of assuming an idea expressed by one of Shakespeare's characters is also Shakespeare's. Instead I insist that Hamlet's opinion is also Shakespeare's because this idea pervades the very form and content of Shakespeare's work.

Appreciation for Shakespeare traditionally rests on detaching his work from the language; on confirming that Shakespeare is more than *simply* a poet. Technically speaking, Shakespeare was not merely a poet. He was a dramatist who wrote poetic plays with vibrant characters and engaging plots. Even poems such as *Venus and Adonis* (and *Shakespeare's Sonnets*) are composed primarily of dialogue, i.e. speech. But speech is language, and – especially in a medieval context – speech is rhetoric. And Shakespeare, himself a rhetorician, would have considered human speech to be the primary element of his work.

How can I be so presumptuous as to claim I can peer into Shakespeare's mind? Well it's not an unusual thing to do, these days. There are numerous literary critiques of Shakespeare based on conjecture, as the facts we have about the life of the man from Stratford are sparse. Shakespeare critics routinely base their analysis on conjecture about Shakespeare's imagined biography, personality and moods.

Take Henry J. Paul's book, *The Royal Play of Macbeth*, which was the accepted wisdom on the Scottish play for many years. Paul decrees that the first three acts of *Macbeth* were written precisely "before the end of March 1606"[2] and that he knows for certain "as the dramatist sat at his desk and wrote, he was conscious of the face of the king looking straight at him, so that his words formed themselves to fit this expected audience."[3] The proof that Paul offers for this is purely circumstantial. We have no evidence to support the idea that Shakespeare wrote *Macbeth* with King James in mind.

But facts like don't stop Paul – or anyone else – from fantasizing. There are legions of scholars who imagine they can peer into Shakespeare's mind and read his thoughts. But that is not my method here. Instead I wish to examine the work. There we will find ample proof of Shakespeare's obsession with language. In fact I would posit that the work is as much about language as it is about anything else.

That some would be resistant to this point of view is inevitable. From the start, stage directors and editors modified Shakespeare's text in order to render the language less ambiguous. Today, critics like Harold Bloom are suspicious of anyone who asserts that Shakespeare was primarily a poet. And scholars still waste a lot of time trying to figure out exactly what Shakespeare *means*. Shakespeare was obsessed with the truth that lies in language itself. But truth meant something very different to Shakespeare than it does to us.

As it should have. Truth was his motto, and his last name.

Notes

[1] *Hamlet*, (Folger, 2013) 1.5. 187-88
[2] Paul, Henry N. *The Royal Play of Macbeth*. Octagon Books, 1971. 401
[3] Ibid.

CHAPTER ONE

Bardolatry

Shakespeare's work was not very popular in the years following his death. Even after the reopening of the theatres during The Restoration, Shakespeare's work didn't dominate the stage. In 1668 John Dryden stated that Beaumont and Fletcher were more popular than Shakespeare, and that two of their plays were acted yearly for every one of Shakespeare's. Shakespeare's supremacy was not established until the middle of the 18th century with the advent of bardolatry: until then Shakespeare's reputation was equal to if not less than that of the poets Edmund Spenser and Philip Sidney. Shakespeare's inability to hold the public's attention for the first hundred years after his death is directly related to an attitude to language that invaded England starting in the middle of the 17th century. It is an attitude that persists to this day.

The first meeting of the Royal Society in London was an informal one, in November 1660. They gathered after a lecture by architect Christopher Wren. The society's complete name was "The Royal Society of London for the Improving Natural Knowledge," and their motto was "Nullius in verba." A colloquial translation would be "take nobody's word for it."

It's important not to underestimate the significant of this motto. Ostensibly the organization was dedicated to practical experimentation as a testing ground for facts, and it is usually taken for granted that the focus of the Royal Society was to ensure that practical experiments were useful, taking its cue from Francis Bacon whom they celebrated as a spiritual, if not actual founder. Isaac Newton became a member of the organization in 1703, which wished to serve as a model for the state in terms of function.

So "Nullius in verba" says it all. The motto represented a major cultural shift – from trusting words – to a scepticism about them, and from a fictional representation of the natural world to direct observation of the real world before our eyes.

So the Royal Society concerned itself not only with practical experimentation, but with the policing of language. Simultaneously as they urged people to turn to the real world and perceive its functions through the senses, they turned people away from art – or a certain type of art. And though they didn't mention Shakespeare specifically, Shakespeare's work – and all poetry in the manner of Shakespeare – was in the Royal Society's crosshairs.

Richard Nate speaks of Margaret Cavendish (1623-73), an aristocrat and a writer, who tried her hand at both philosophy and fiction. Although she was not a member of the Royal Society (and of course was scorned by them, because she was a woman), her musings were very often concerned with the society's philosophical ideas. In a story about an Empress who confronts the "parrot-men," Cavendish dramatizes her own objections to the poets of her day, neatly summarizing the Royal Society's attitude to poetic language:

> [T]he Empress appeared not a little troubled, and told them [the parrot-men], that they followed too much the rules of art, and confounded themselves with too nice formalities and distinctions; but since I know, said she, that you are a people who have naturally voluble tongues, and good memories; I desire you to consider more the subject you speak of, than your artificial periods, connexions and parts of speech, and leave the rest to your natural eloquence; which they did, and so became very eminent orators.[1]

In his essay on Cavendish, Nate summarizes the Royal Society's pervasive influence: "In 1666, however, the boundaries between science and literature had become more stable due to the efforts of the Royal Society, which not only argued against figurative language but also demanded a clear distinction between the products of reason and the products of the imagination."[2] Nate goes on to suggest that this attitude to art that dominated the early modern scientific community was hostile: "The early modern scientists' distrust of the imagination has almost become a commonplace."[3]

A scepticism about poetry that was "artificial" and dominated by excessive figurative language not only dominated the Royal Society, but by the end of the 18th century it permeated English society as a whole. Poets themselves were also concerned with "use." Wit for its own sake was scorned, and comedy came to be seen as dangerous if it was not corrective and gentle. Taves speaks of the poet/playwright Joseph Addison criticizing the use of "similitudes, odd metaphor, conceit, epigrammatic turns as mere juggling wit, fancy – amusing fancy without regard for truth"[4] Addison's contemporary Corbyn Morris made a distinction between humour and wit, and preferred the former over the later:

> Humour is *Nature*, or what really appears in the Subject, without any Embellishments; Wit only a Stroke of *Art*, where the Subject being insufficient of itself, is garnished and deck'd with auxiliary Objects … Humour is more interesting than Wit in general as the *Oddities* and *Foibles* of *Persons* in *real Life* are more apt to affect our Passions, than any Oppositions or Relations between *inanimate* Objects.[5]

And Willibald Ruch speaks of the same shift in attitudes: "A term became necessary for the humanitarian, tolerant, and benevolent forms of laughter … Humour received a philosophical twist, e.g. Samuel Taylor Coleridge (1792-1843) stated that humour arises 'whenever the finite is contemplated in reference to the infinite.'"[6]

Who would suggest that Shakespeare's work is not human, or that it does not contemplate the relationship between the finite and the infinite? Well one man who wished to popularize

Shakespeare's work in the volatile literary atmosphere of the mid-1700's was certainly worried that Shakespeare's work displayed an overabundance of wit, and that it lacked a good old-fashioned moral compass. David Garrick (1717-1779) – a renowned actor and theatre manager – is famous for introducing Shakespeare as a popular dramatist to the 18th century theatregoing public. His productions of Shakespeare plays – where he himself often played the leading roles – were much acclaimed. The productions not only made Shakespeare exceedingly popular, but turned him into an object of worship. Cunningham quotes Susan Green describing Garrick's Ode to Shakespeare (upon the erection of a statue to Shakespeare in Stratford, 1796): "Most scholars agree that English Bardolatry was affirmed when Garrick held his grandiose, but hilariously tawdry deification of the Bard at his jubilee."[7] Cunningham's summary of the actual content of the Ode (a speech accompanied – recitative style – by music) is revealing:

> Shakespeare is celebrated for his 'wonder-teeming mind' and ability to 'raise other worlds and beings' (lines 66-67). He is nature's heir, admired for his control of the 'subject passions' (line 81) Shakespeare even has the god-like power to force the 'guilty lawless tribe' (line 102), like Claudius to confess concealed sins 'Out bursts the penitential tear!/ The look appall'd the crime reveals' (lines 108-109). Shakespeare ('first of poets, best of men,' line 288) is a moral force for good.[8]

There was no doubt about it; in order to popularize Shakespeare Garrick was compelled to represent him as less an artificial versifier than an arbiter of morals, as less a manipulator of words than a teacher of men. To do this, Garrick set out to rewrite the plays. His primary task was to ensure that each of the sinful characters he played had a suitably repentant Christian demise, including the all-important repentant final speech. His second task was to excise Shakespeare's obsessive wordplay. Garrick considered it unnecessary and offensive. Cunningham tells us that Garrick's problem with *Romeo and Juliet* was the 'quibbles.' A quibble was defined as "low conceit depending on the sound of words; a pun."[9] Much of the sexual joking in *Romeo and Juliet* had to be removed for "the majority of critics of the 18th century deplored Shakespeare's wordplay."[10]

Nowadays we generally view rewriting Shakespeare's plays as something akin to heresy – except occasionally when avant-garde directors fiddle, controversially, with the text. But our present seeming reverence for the text does not originate from our *love for language* itself. In fact editors and literary critics treat Shakespeare's work not as poetry, but as reasoning, not as *fancy* but as *learning*. They are not as interested in its persuasive or poetic effect as they are convinced that there is a single meaning to the work that must be uncovered; a meaning that exists beyond, or even in spite of, the poetry. The scrupulous method that characterizes most Shakespeare scholarship is to weigh one version of each play against another.

Once scholars have calculated the word that was actually intended by Shakespeare (which can be a difficult job considering early modern variant spellings), critics then proceed to focus on each separate word in *exegetical* – not *poetical* – fashion. In practice this means relentlessly examining each word, discerning its etymology and likely usage in the early modern period, noting Shakespeare's other uses of the word – as well as placing the word in context of the sentence where it is used. Scholars then proceed to argue over the 'true meaning' of the passage. This ignores one of the primary features of poetical language in general and of early modern poetry in particular: the polysemous nature of words.

The fact is that poets use language in a connotative – not denotative – way. Poetic language may have many meanings, and is expected to be allusive and resonant. Common, conversational denotative speech is expected to be exact, truthful and useful, and the extraneous, accidental or hidden connotations one may find in it do not serve day to day human communication. (In other words, it does not help me purchase oranges at a grocery store if the clerk thinks I am using 'oranges' as a metaphor).

I'm not suggesting that Shakespeare's work has no meaning, or that it is hopeless to consider that meaning. Musing on meanings, discussing meaning, 'feeling' the meaning – intuiting conflicting meanings – this is a truly poetic experience, and not at all exact. In contrast, pinning down the message that was intended by the author is a kind of literary science, and not poetic at all. Roland Barthes evocatively describes the experience of connotative language in *The Pleasure of the Text*: "My pleasure can very well take the form of a drift. *Drifting* occurs whenever *I do not respect the whole*, and whenever, by dint of seeming driven about by language's illusions, seductions, and intimidations, like a cork on the waves, I remain motionless, pivoting on the *intractable* bliss that binds me to the text (to the world)."[11]

In 1066 the Normans invaded England and French was the language spoken by the ruling class for nearly 300 years. Latin was the language of the church. During Shakespeare's time, the English language as we know it today was in development, still incorporating French words – and English was often referred to as 'the vulgar' and thought to be somewhat inappropriate, not only for church services, but for poetry. There were no authoritative universal dictionaries as we know them, and it is common knowledge that some of the words Shakespeare used were invented by Shakespeare himself. Shakespeare coined 1700 words (among them: *academe, eyeball, equivocal, hobnob* and *amazement*). Early modern English was very fluid and in flux, and often there were no stable meanings.

Harold Bloom is the Garrick of our day – he speaks to the modern man on the street about Shakespeare in a manner that anyone can understand. Bloom popularizes Shakespeare through his critical works like *Shakespeare: The Invention of the Human*, by downplaying Shakespeare's wordplay (i.e. his ambiguity) and emphasizing his moral meanings (his truth). Bloom is shrewd, and he understands that the idea of a language-based appreciation of Shakespeare must be discarded if one wishes to turn Shakespeare into a God: "There are two contradictory ways to account for Shakespeare's eminence. If, for you, literature is primarily language, then the primacy of Shakespeare is only a cultural phenomenon, produced by socio-political urgencies."[12]

In an introduction to a collection of essays on Shakespeare, Bloom clearly sets the sonnets below the plays because they are composed mainly of language, and are not drama: "The poetic achievement of the Sonnets has just enough of the playwright's uncanny power to show that we confront the same writer, but the awesome cognitive originality and psychological persuasiveness of the major dramas are subdued in all but a few of the sequences."[13]

Bloom characterizes Shakespeare's writing as 'secular scripture,' and quotes Owen Barfield: "There is a very real sense, humiliating as it may seem, in which what we generally venture to call our feelings are really Shakespeare's 'meaning.'"[14] Certainly any work comparable to the Bible is necessarily required to provide us with a staunch moral compass, and any work which creates our feelings is Godlike. Any way you look at it, Bloom posits that we need to be more human (hence the title of his magnum opus) and Shakespeare's work can teach us how.

Bloom's reasons for preferring the character Falstaff above all other Shakespearean characters reveals a moral criterion: "Many of us become machines for fulfilling responsibilities; Falstaff is the largest and best reproach we can find. I am aware that I commit the original Sin that all historicists – of all generations – decry, joined by all formalists as well. I exalt Falstaff above his plays."[15] Bloom is suggesting the character of Falstaff offers a moral lesson for us all, transcending language, and exemplifying what Bloom calls 'the human.' And this suggestion that Shakespeare's finest characters help us to be our best selves is bolstered by his idea that "Shakespeare became the greatest master at exploiting the void between persons and the personal ideal."[16]

In other words Shakespeare helps us understand how to realize our best selves. And our best self is – despite all his flaws – a character very much like Falstaff. Bloom says Shakespeare must certainly have been a man who was "affable and shrewd"[17] which pretty much describes Falstaff. It's easy to imagine God as a Falstaffian sort of guy – a bit overweight and jolly – fun to be with; but smart as a fox.

Bloom also famously attributes the attractiveness of Shakespeare's characters to their inwardness – which was a bold innovation for the early modern period: "inner selves do not abound in Shakespeare's contemporaries."[18] Bloom imagines Shakespeare to be perhaps the very first novelist, creating the modern concept of our inner selves. I do not question the universality of Shakespeare's characters, or his superlative skill at crafting convincing, moving characters. But there is much medieval and early modern writing that displays humanity, that appeals to our best selves, and creates deep emotion, but which does not touch us the way Shakespeare's work does.

One thinks of Chaucer, Marlowe – or Ben Jonson. These writers created characters that – despite their somewhat one dimensional qualities – nevertheless speak to us directly. So what is the one aspect of Shakespeare's characters that separates them from ordinary flawed comic characters in a Ben Jonson farce, or

Marlowe's Faust, or one of the riders on the trip to Canterbury? It is Shakespeare's poetry. Shakespeare's characters speak with an extremely well-crafted combination of eloquence, and – what used to be described in the early modern period as 'decorum.' All of Shakespeare's characters speak beautifully and/or eloquently, but they also speak in a manner that is suitable for their particular personalities, following the 'decorum' of that character in their words.

I would suggest that, if examine your responses to Shakespeare's characters, you will discover that what intrigues you and touches you is not their inwardness, but the language they use to speak about themselves, which gives the *illusion* of inwardness. Take away that language and they are not only no longer Shakespearean characters. They are much more like the rest of the characters in early modern literature. I am not suggesting, for instance, that Hamlet is not intensely introspective – but what makes that introspection seem profound is *the way it is expressed*. Even those characters that are not superficially sympathetic are made so by their eloquence.

For instance, characters like Caliban, Jaques and Shylock are essentially variations on a theme: they are the outsider characters in comedies (*The Merchant of Venice* and *The Tempest* are both comic in form, though sometimes described as romances or problem plays). At the end of these plays these three lonely, bitter characters do not pair off like all the young lovers do, but are left, significantly, alone. Caliban and Shylock are labelled as evil repeatedly, and Jaques is perhaps the quintessential 'other.' Yet though all three are alone and somewhat malignant, they are certainly etched convincingly and flawed in a believable, human way – a way that makes us laugh, and/or disturbs us.

But what makes the characters complete – unique and profound – is their eloquence. It is their observations about the world and themselves that convince us of a piercing humanity. Shylock, Jaques and Caliban have some of the most beautiful lines in Shakespeare: Shylock: "Hath not a Jew eyes?"[19]; Jacques: "All the world's a stage, / And all the men merely players"[20]; Caliban: "When I waked, I cried to dream again."[21]

I would go so far as to argue that Shakespeare's characters *are* language. A perfect example would be Cleopatra (in *Antony and Cleopatra*) and Venus (in the poem *Venus and Adonis*). In the early modern context, there was nothing morally attractive about these two women. They are both beautiful, but their beauty enslaves men and destroys them. In the early modern period the dominant paradigm was the notion that women's sexuality was so overpowering that it might destroy men, Antony's extreme love for Cleopatra would have seemed alienating and emasculating. In fact to such an audience the subject matter of *Antony and Cleopatra* would have seemed more like the stuff of farce or satire than tragedy. This is perhaps the origin of Cleopatra's dire prediction that some day an amateur transvestite will play her on stage: "I shall see some squeaking Cleopatra boy my greatness i' the posture of a whore."[22] This speaks to the tremendous challenge of creating sympathy for a character who would surely have seemed – to the average early modern theatregoer – not merely a whore, but a destroyer of men.

Nevertheless Shakespeare does create sympathy for Cleopatra. But I would suggest that Cleopatra is not sympathetic to us because of Shakespeare's great psychological insight. Yes Cleopatra is a 'real' woman with desires and fears, which we recognize, and which make us feel close to her. But what transforms her into a profound tragic heroine is her poetry – as when she remembers her great lover, Antony, so poignantly after his death: "His face was the heavens, and therein stuck / a sun and moon which kept their course and / lighted / the little 'O' the earth."[23]

From Garrick to Bloom, those who seek to celebrate Shakespeare have done so at the cost of de-emphasizing the importance of his language. Why is it so important to emphasize Shakespeare's Godlike omniscience and conscience, instead of the power of his poetry, his 'wit'? The answer must begin with a search for Shakespeare, the man.

Notes

[1] Nate, Richard, "'Plain and Vulgarly Express'd': Margaret Cavendish and the Discourse of the New Science." *Rhetorica: A Journal of History of Rhetoric* 19.4 2001, 412

[2] Ibid., 415

[3] Ibid.

[4] Taves, Stuart M. *The Amiable Humourist*. University of Chicago Press, 1960. 58-59

[5] Morris, Corbyn. "Falstaff's Humour," *William Shakespeare: The Critical Heritage Vol 3 1733-1752* Routledge, 1995. 123

[6] Ruch, Willibald. *The Sense of Humor*, Walter de Gruyter, 2007. 8-9

[7] Cunningham, Vanessa. *Shakespeare and Garrick*. Cambridge University Press, 2008. 107

[8] Ibid., 110

[9] Ibid., 64

[10] Ibid., 65

[11] Barthes, Roland. *The Pleasure of the Text*, Hill and Wang, 1975, 18

[12] Bloom, Harold. *Shakespeare: The Invention of the Human*, Riverhead Books, 1998. 16

[13] Bloom, Harold (ed.). *Shakespeare's Poems and Sonnets*, 9

[14] Bloom, Harold. *Shakespeare: Invention of the Human*, 12-13

[15] Ibid., 313-314.

[16] Ibid., 7

[17] Ibid., 8

[18] Ibid., 1

[19] *The Merchant of Venice*. (Signet Classic, 1965) 3.1 55-56

[20] *As You Like It*. (Folger, 1997) 2.3 146-147

[21] *The Tempest*. (Folger, 2015) 3.2 155-56

[22] *Antony and Cleopatra*. (Folger, 1999) 5.2 266-268

[23] *Antony and Cleopatra*. (Folger, 1999) 5.2 97-100

CHAPTER TWO

Identity

Who was Shakespeare? The answer to this question is usually: "Who cares? I love Shakespeare's plays. I don't need to know how he liked his coffee in the morning. In fact knowing that might ruin it all for me." I might agree if this objection wasn't based on a fundamental falsehood. We think we are not conscious of Shakespeare the man when we read the plays, but the truth is what we have is scant knowledge based on scant facts, which deeply affects our perception of the work. There is much common knowledge about the man that is taken for granted. Not only does it influence how we read Shakespeare's work, but it is a primary force shaping our conception of what a great writer should be. Shakespeare was the greatest English-language writer of all time, *ergo*, any great writer must himself be a person like Shakespeare.

So who was the "man from Stratford"? Ben Jonson said of Shakespeare "and though thou hadst small Latin and less Greek."[1] This has been taken to mean that Shakespeare was somewhat uneducated. Some have argued over Jonson's syntax. Jonson the poet – like most early modern writers – was ambiguous and allusive – and enigmatic, especially when speaking of Shakespeare. Did he mean that Shakespeare had a small knowledge of Latin and less knowledge of Greek? Or is the sentence in the subjunctive mode, i.e. does it really mean – if Shakespeare had *happened to have* "small Latin and less Greek" – *which he didn't* – *then* Jonson would *still* have praised him? It doesn't really matter; one doesn't need Jonson's encomium to conclude that Shakespeare – as we imagine him anyway – was uneducated.

Shakespeare's "profession" should be enough to answer any questions about his education. He was, according to legend, a part-time writer. The primary profession of the man from Stratford was grain merchant and landowner. Most of the records that we have about Shakespeare – outside of his will – (and his name on lists as both a performer and an investor in London theatre) are from lawsuits. These lawsuits deal with contracts, disputes, and money-lending. If one examines these documents with a certain diligence (and many scholars have) one gets the impression that Shakespeare spent a lot of time in court, and was nothing if not a pecuniary person. But in his spare time, Shakespeare somehow found time to become the greatest writer that ever lived. There is no proof that the man from Stratford attended university or even grammar school, and since he was a glover's son who aspired to be a grain merchant and landowner, why would he bother?

The details of Shakespeare's biography are a liberal mix of fact and fiction. But need we separate the two? What matters is who we *imagine* Shakespeare to be. Some of what we think we know about Shakespeare comes from one of his earliest biographers, Nicholas Rowe, whose ground-breaking edition of Shakespeare's plays in 1709 is important not so much because we can verify the biographical details contained in it, but because most of what Rowe said about Shakespeare has stuck. For instance, Rowe claims Shakespeare was convicted of deer stealing, and that as an actor, he played the ghost of Hamlet's father.

Neither of these "facts" are true. Nevertheless, they fit our imagining of who Shakespeare was; a rustic sort of fellow, with – not so much a criminal profile – as a natural tendency towards boyish mischievousness. The "fact" that Shakespeare played the ghost of Hamlet's father seems like poetic justice. After all, the man from Stratford had a son called *Hamnet*, who died at age 11. It is commonly thought that *Hamlet* is a play about Hamnet, or at least it is a play written in memory of his tragic death. How touching and appropriate it would have been for Shakespeare to have played Hamlet's father in the famous play.

This detail is like so many we have collected about Shakespeare; it points to the idea that he had a family life with the usual bumps in the road, but one that was nevertheless not *overly* crowded with incident. Everyone knows that his wife, Ann Hathaway, was six years older than he. This could be considered, I think, one of those 'little bumps' on the highway of life. It is not of course objectionable or even incomprehensible to us that a man might marry an older woman. Yet it is *slightly* out of the ordinary for a wife to be six years older than her husband, and it has led to much speculation about whether Shakespeare's wife trapped him into marriage (was she somewhat of a Lady Macbeth?) or seduced him (was she the inspiration for *Venus and Adonis*?). Or was his love for this older woman conflicted (*Shakespeare's Sonnets*)?

Then there is the added detail that Shakespeare disappeared from his marriage for a time. One must deal with the years 1578-82 and 1585-92 – sometimes called "the lost years." During these years there is suddenly no record of Shakespeare's business transactions. It seems reasonable to conclude that he may have run off to London, or (as Stephen Greenblatt suggests) with the travelling theatre company The Queen's Men. And if Shakespeare were to leave his family for a total of eleven years, it might suggest that there were tensions in the marriage.

All of this sounds reasonable. The only problem is, there is no basis for it in reality. We have no proof that the man from Stratford left his wife and joined a theatre troupe because he was having marital problems – all we know is that we have no record of him for 11 years, other than his name attached to some theatrical pursuits. But again, I am not so much interested in criticizing scholars for basing their biographies of Shakespeare completely on conjecture; I am much more interested in the picture of the man that this conjecture paints for us.

Was this Shakespeare of our imagining an unconventional man? Leaving one's wife and children might be considered unconventional, but then again it might not. To shed more light on the situation there is the issue of the Shakespeare family coat of arms. It has long been noted that Shakespeare's father aspired to be a gentleman, and to that end had attempted to acquire a coat of arms. Recently it has been affirmed that the man from Stratford *himself* also desired the much cherished "gentleman status," and worked to get the coat of arms his father had been unable to get – only to face opposition because he worked in the theatre.

This detail about the man from Stratford suggests that, even if his marriage was a bit odd, and if he held the not so respectable position of part-time writer for, and player in, the theatre, he nevertheless held values in common with regular middle class people. After all, he aspired to be one of them – a "gentleman."

The one thing that is truly unconventional about this imagining of Shakespeare is his enormous writing talent, especially as we have no proof of the man from Stratford's education. Was Shakespeare a genius? It used to be assumed that the primary factor in genius was IQ. Recently, researchers like Malcolm Gladwell and Dean Simonton have concluded that a high IQ is not good enough; you need hard work. So Shakespeare may very well have worked his way to the top.

What can we conclude, if we put together all of the details that form our present suppositions about Shakespeare's life?

Well, most importantly, we can conclude that the Shakespeare we know and love was an ordinary man – a man who is easy for us to understand and relate to. A kind of exemplary ordinary man, in fact – as he fits the profile of an aspiring capitalist, perfectly. What does "ordinary" mean to us, exactly? It means "just like you and me." Many men are uneducated (even getting a university education these days means you might be uneducated, as, increasingly, a university degree is just a piece of paper that will get you a job). Many men work in business, and have hobbies (such as the fishing, sports, stamp collecting or dabbling in the arts). Many men have basically stable marriages that are only rocky now and then. Most middle class people work hard. When it comes down to it, Shakespeare was the same as you and I. The corollary? When it finally comes down to it, *anyone could be Shakespeare.*

I would suggest that this vision of Shakespeare – despite being somewhat unlikely – is very, very appealing.

I am not suggesting that there has been a conspiracy to make Shakespeare appear to be a common man. It could have come about quite naturally. After all, it's only natural that in the late 1700s – when Shakespeare first became the Godlike figure he is today – critics and biographers would want to shape God in the image of themselves. The late 18th century was a time when capitalism was on the rise, when society was no longer made up simply of aristocrats and the very poor – but also of a burgeoning middle class. It was a time when humour was favoured if it was gentler, and language was policed by the Royal Society if it was over-embellished. It was a time when people were beginning to believe that anyone might have a successful life if they worked hard enough.

Shakespeare actually lived in a very different period – the early modern (post-medieval) period when society was still feudal. Writing was, if anything, over embellished, and life was, as Thomas Hobbes observed in 1651 "nasty, brutish and short."[2] There was little hope of "rising" in society and if one did rise, one would be viewed with suspicion.

I would suggest that it is only natural that we have preferred a Shakespeare who is not only Godlike in his powers but (how flattering to us all) compatible with our own lives and aspirations. The only problem with this imagining of Shakespeare – as pleasant and hopeful as it is – is not so much that it doesn't match up to the facts (though generally speaking it doesn't) but – whatever the truth of our imaginings – they shape not only our view of Shakespeare, but our view of what any great writer should be.

For the truth about great artists generally is that they tend not to be ordinary. This is not because they are Gods, but because, on the contrary, they are all too human. They tend to be complex people who lead difficult lives. This stereotype has at least a glancing relationship to the facts (as most stereotypes do). Think of Van Gogh's ear, Picasso's misogyny, Sylvia Plath's suicide, Jack Kerouac's alcoholism, Beethoven's deafness, Tchaikovsky's homosexuality, Georgia O'Keefe's, well … vaginas … the list goes on and on.

Due to Shakespeare's distance from us in time, and due to bardolatry, he has some how slipped under the wire – he is a singular artist for being remembered as an ordinary, very moral man, and an aspiring capitalist. This is why he is so universally respected. Shakespeare's "identifiability" explains why families who would never go closer to Shakespeare's work than *Shakespeare in Love* make the trek to Stratford, and why he is assumed to be the greatest writer that ever lived. It's why there's no stopping "Our Shakespeare." If there ever was an artist tailor-made for philistines, Shakespeare is it.

And yet I remember – as a teenage assistant store clerk at Shoppers Drug Mart in Toronto – having a conversation with my boss about Shakespeare. He knew I was a theatre geek, so he told me about his trip to Stratford, Ontario. "We went to see two plays," he said. "*Hello Dolly* and *Much Ado About Nothing*. *Hello Dolly* was great, really really liked it. When it comes to *Much Ado About Nothing* …" – he leaned over and smiled at me wryly – "well – it was." This is the same voice that says: "If that's what he meant, why didn't he just come out and say it?" My boss was certainly willing to pay a visit to Stratford, Ontario, but it was unlikely he would actually understand or – God forbid – *enjoy* Shakespeare's work.

Yet academics carry on with pointless research that exists within the artist-as-aspiring-capitalist paradigm. Academics tie themselves in knots to reassure us that Shakespeare's plays are not strange or incomprehensible, or really, after all, from another era – they are like 20th century tragedies, or even Broadway musicals. Joseph Candido in the recent *Shakespeare the Man* paints a picture of Shakespeare as a "Willy Loman-esque" figure. He says "the vibrant world of monetary exchange was one, moreover to which the young William Shakespeare was unusually close."[3] If Hamlet is to be examined only through a modern lens then we must somehow assume that he is, in some way, a small-time businessman.

R.S. White goes much further and suggests (also in *Shakespeare the Man*) that Shakespeare may have been a kind of enterprising, proto-capitalist troubadour, trying to sell his wares – and that *Shakespeare's Sonnets* are the result of this entrepreneurial ingenuity: Shakespeare longed to write a "successful long prose romance with embedded songs, sonnets, elegies, complaints and other poems which would hit the fashion and make some money [so] … he devised a story linking several fictional characters."[4] The sonnets are thus confusing and tantalizing not because they are strangely personal or have a hidden meaning, but because Shakespeare – on the lam from his farm in Stratford and unable to pay for lodgings in London – needed some extra money and didn't have time to finish them.

Maintaining the myth of this "just-an-ordinary-man-like-you" Shakespeare has become de rigeur, so much so that scholars inevitably commence their analysis by referring to the (very few) details they can find about Shakespeare's life (usually his money troubles) trying to relate the content of his work to that.

What would happen if we reversed this paradigm? What would happen if we tried to find the real man in the work, instead of trying to understand the work through the man?

We avoid doing this for one very simple reason: The New Criticism. This highly influential literary movement was officially inaugurated in 1941 with John Ransom's book of the same name. It is an approach to English literature characterized by concentration on the text. The New Criticism vilified any attempt to extrapolate information about the author – or the author's intention – from the work. The New Criticism's William Wimsatt is credited with coining the term "intentional fallacy": the notion that we might be able to discover the author's intent, or biography, from the work.

T.S. Eliot was one of the founders of the New Criticism. His opinion of *Hamlet* is fascinating. Hamlet is probably the most famous character in English literature. But Eliot rejects the play because he thinks it is not art; it is confession. He thinks that Shakespeare was not able to find an "objective correlative" for his personal thoughts and feelings, and that the play, instead of being poetry, is confusing and embarrassingly personal. I think that Eliot's reasons for disliking the play have a lot to do with why people like the play so much, why it is considered by many to be their favourite Shakespeare play. But it also has to do with what we have been afraid of learning, and persist in being afraid of learning – about Shakespeare the man.

For Eliot, *Hamlet* is simply an anomaly: "More people have thought *Hamlet* a work of art because they found it interesting than have found it interesting because it is a work of art."[5] He suggests that the appeal of *Hamlet*, like the Mona Lisa, lies not so much in its artistry, as in its oddness. He states that the play is an "artistic failure." He says that an analysis of the play reveals something dark about Shakespeare's character that should not be examined too closely. "*Hamlet*, like *The Sonnets*, is full of some stuff that the writer could not drag to light, contemplate or manipulate into art."[6] Eliot blasts the play's inability to find a proper narrative to express its ideas, specifically the inadequacy of its action: "Nothing that Shakespeare can do with the plot can express Hamlet for him."[7]

Eliot is alarmed to find Shakespeare, the man, in Hamlet, and along with his colleague Wimsatt he is intent on erasing from our consciousness the notion that great art should ever reveal the artist. The notion that all great writing must feature an invisible author seems to have been inaugurated by Shakespeare critics. It seems to me that this may have happened *because* of Shakespeare. Certainly literary critics have traditionally gone out of their way to assure us that Shakespeare – the man – is invisible in his work.

Ben Jonson's introduction to the first folio of 1623 advised famously "reader, look, / not on his picture, but his book."[8] Writing in the early 1800s Hazlitt attributed Shakespeare's greatness to his ability encompass all points of view: "The striking peculiarity of Shakespeare's mind was its generic quality, its power of communication with all other minds – so that it contained a universe of thought and feeling within itself, and has no one peculiar bias, or exclusive excellence more than another."[9] Bardolators Garrick and Bloom make it clear that Shakespeare's genius encompasses all men. Bloom reminds us "as a playwright Shakespeare seems too wise to believe anything,"[10] and ... "his politics like his religion, evades me, but I think he was too wary to have any."[11]

And yet there is nothing essentially *true* about the notion that the greatness of an author's work can be measured by its distance from the personality of the author. There are great writers whose work was semi-autobiographical and/or personal; Proust, Plath, Lorca, Tennessee Williams (and many more) come to mind.

Generally speaking, a great author can – and often does – reveal him or herself in their work. So what is it about Shakespeare's life that might have caused critics from the beginning, to fear its appearance in his work, and specifically in the character of Hamlet?

Hamlet is a young prince. He has just come back from school in Wittenberg, Germany. He is also a stage director; with a company of actors that he asks to perform a play that he hopes will implicate the new King Claudius, his stepfather, in the murder of his father. The plot of *Hamlet* – or what there is of it – revolves around Hamlet's inability to enact revenge, and throughout the play he is trying to convince himself to act. The subplots, though somewhat incidental to this primary conflict, involve two actions. The first action is Claudius' plot to kill Hamlet, and the second is Hamlet's possible betrothal to a young woman (Ophelia) who is the daughter of the Claudius's advisor (Polonius). Claudius sends Hamlet on a trip to Europe and orders two men (Rosencrantz and Guildenstern) to kill him. Hamlet survives, but he is set upon by pirates and lands naked on the shores of Denmark. Hamlet's romantic entanglement with Ophelia is fraught. He verbally abuses her. She commits suicide when he is away in Europe, and he is heartbroken to learn of her suicide when he returns.

There was a man in early modern England whose life resembled the details of Hamlet's life to a startling degree. His name was Edward de Vere. As the Earl of Oxford, Edward de Vere was one of the richest nobles in England from one of the premier bloodlines in in the land, second only in nobility to Queen Elizabeth. He was born in 1550. De Vere's father – like Hamlet's father – died when he was young. De Vere was sent to live with William Cecil (as a ward of Queen Elizabeth). Just as Polonius is an advisor to Claudius and father to Ophelia (romantically involved with Hamlet), William Cecil was an advisor to Queen Elizabeth and father to Ann Cecil (romantically involved with Edward de Vere).

Hamlet accuses Ophelia of infidelity and she commits suicide, which Hamlet regrets. De Vere also accused Ann Cecil of infidelity, only to later find out after her early death, that she was probably innocent. Like Hamlet. De Vere travelled to Europe (and visited educational institutions in Germany, as Hamlet did). And also, as in the play, when de Vere returned from Europe he was set upon by pirates and landed "naked" on the shore. Hamlet is said to be a kind of early modern fashion-plate – the "glass of fashion and the mold of form."[12] De Vere, similarly, was infamous for his ostentatious Italianate dress. And finally de Vere, like Prince Hamlet, had a company of actors – they were called Oxford's Men.

Co-incidence you say? Perhaps. Or perhaps the man from Stratford knew the Earl of Oxford and was writing about him? Perhaps. But certainly the notion that a nobleman like de Vere was Shakespeare would have been repellent to early modern audiences. Nobleman were not expected to do the lowly and still somewhat scandalous job of playwriting. The public theatres in London, after all, were located outside the city limits so that they could be close to the brothels.

But also there was de Vere's scandalous personal life. As a young he may have "accidentally" murdered someone in a quarrel. De Vere was not only a womanizer, but he imported a "castrato" from Italy to sing for the queen. This young man arrived after de Vere returned from Europe and de Vere was consequently accused by his enemies of sodomizing him. Most significantly, perhaps, de Vere died in disgrace – possibly in debauchery – having squandered his vast fortune, one of the largest in England.

All of this might explain why Shakespeare's contemporaries might have wanted to pretend that the man who wrote *Hamlet was not writing about himself.* This might explain why Ben Jonson would have warned us not to look at the man himself, and why Nicholas Rowe would have written such a fanciful biography of him that was mostly untrue.

Eliot thinks that the play never finds an action that is a satisfactory objective correlative, and that the play is, as a result, not only embarrassingly confessional, but unclear. I would suggest that the play is certainly unclear, even mysterious – and deliberately so. Hamlet resists action not because he is a coward (though he accuses himself of this), or because he doesn't love his father, or because he is immoral. He doesn't avenge his father simply because he would rather talk about the issue than act. It is usually suggested that Hamlet must choose between action and inaction. I would suggest that the choice before him is between action and rhetoric.

Hamlet mostly just talks – quite artfully, and poetically, and sometimes nonsensically. He plays with words and manipulates language in ways that are subtle, and he is so good at that manipulation that we are not certain if he is telling the truth or not. Hamlet lives in his imagination more than he does in the real world. That Hamlet lives in his imagination is confirmed by the language he uses; he speaks incoherently, using puns and allusions and – it seems sometimes – irrelevancies. It is an issue in the play whether Hamlet is mad or if he is feigning madness; Hamlet is in this sense, an artist. In *Midsummer Night's Dream* Shakespeare proposes a special superiority for the lover, the madman and the poet all because they can "apprehend more than cool reason comprehends."[13]

Eliot alludes to the "darkness" that he finds so repellent in the play, the personal matter(s) that he thinks the playwright might have been afraid to bring to light. I think what is actually happening here is that Shakespeare has painted an accurate portrait of himself, and that he was, to some degree, a typical courtier of Elizabeth's early modern England, who saw himself – like so many courtiers of the period who had read Castiglione's *The Book of the Courtier* – as being more of a poet than a man of action. But Shakespeare, like Hamlet, ultimately chose writing poetry over making war.

Why suggest this? In 1578 Gabriel Harvey delivered a speech in honour of the Edward de Vere, the Earl of Oxford, at a celebration at Cambridge University. De Vere was only 28 years old, and had recently returned from a tour of Europe:

> Thy splendid fame, great earl, demands even more than the case of others the services of a poet possessing lofty eloquence. Thy merit doth not creep along the ground, nor can it be confined within the limits of song. It is a wonder that reaches as far as the heavenly orbs ... For a long time past Phoebus Apollo has cultivated thy mind in the arts. English poetical measure have been sung by thee long enough. Let that Courtly Epistle – more polished even than the writings of Castiglione himself – ... witness how greatly thou does excel in letters. I have seen many Latin verses of thine, yea, even more English verses are extant. Thou hast drunk deep draughts not only of the Muses of France and Italy, but has learned the manners of many men, and the arts of foreign countries. It was not for nothing that Sturmius himself was visited by thee. Neither in France, Italy, nor Germany are any such cultivated and polished men. O thou hero worthy of renown, throw away the insignificant pen, throw away the bloodless books and writings that serve no useful purpose. Now must the sword be brought into play. Now is the time for thee to sharpen thy spear and to handle great engines of war ... In thy breast is noble blood, Courage animates thy brow, Mars lives thy tongue, Minerva strengthens thy right hand, Bellona reigns in thy body, within thee burns the fires of Mars. Thine eyes flash fire, thy will shakes spears. Who would not swear that Achilles had come to life again?[14]

There is much that is significant in this speech, and so much that is intentionally veiled. Harvey's ode to de Vere seems congratulatory – he speaks of him as a great artist and rhetorician – "a poet possessing lofty eloquence" and "a wonder which reaches as far as the heavenly orbs." Harvey also mentions de Vere's visit to Johannes Sturm, who was the most celebrated teacher of rhetoric in Europe. But Harvey demands that Oxford stop being a poet (and playwright): "throw away the insignificant pen, throw away the bloodless books, and writings that serve no useful purpose, now must the sword be brought into play. Now is the time for thee to sharpen the spear and handle great engines of war." Could it be any more clear that Harvey is addressing Hamlet? De Vere is a man who must choose between rhetoric and action, and Harvey urges him – nay almost demands – that he choose action.

Those who support de Vere as a candidate for Shakespeare have noted that Harvey refers to "shaking a spear" at the end of his speech, and that this seems to be a veiled reference to what could have been de Vere's pen name as "Shakespeare." It is also certainly possible that Harvey's speech was the inspiration for de Vere to take on this pen name. If de Vere was Hamlet/Shakespeare, then he might not particularly like having been told to put down his pen and take up the sword. He might have ironically taken on the "nom de plume" of "Shake-speare" just to spite Harvey, and of course, to prove that the pen is mightier than the sword.

Harvey's advice to de Vere is just the tip of the iceberg. He is making reference to – but not explicitly speaking of – a prominent rhetorical debate in which Harvey and Oxford were beginning to take separate sides. That he calls de Vere's writing "useless" is also very significant. Harvey was a scholar, and a student of the philosopher Ramus. Ramus' philosophy would some day be at the core of the Royal Society, and all the rhetorical reforms that were to come into vogue in the 17th century – a reformation of language that called for rhetoric that was plainer, practical, and more "useful."

Harvey belonged to one school of thought about rhetoric, and de Vere to another. On Harvey's side was Sidney, and Spenser. On de Vere's side was Nashe, Greene, and John Lyly. In 1579, de Vere and Sidney had a famous quarrel in a tennis court that might have led to a duel (if Queen Elizabeth hadn't intervened). Their argument is often rumoured to have been about poetry. Marshall McLuhan, in his doctoral theses *The Classical Trivium*, suggests that the rivalry between Ramist rhetoricians and old style grammarians was the subject of de Vere and Sidney's quarrel. Their disagreement inspired a later dispute between Nashe and Harvey.

The pamphleteering feud between the old-fashioned stylist Thomas Nashe and the more modern stylist Gabriel Harvey was, McLuhan says, a fight between the humanist school of Erasmus, as represented by Nashe (and associated with Lyly and Edward de Vere, the Earl of Oxford) and Harvey's scholasticism: "The fight between Nashe and Harvey seems to have its origin in the argument between Edward de Vere, Earl of Oxford and Sidney in 1579. Spenser was Ramistic in theology and rhetoric like Sidney, versus the Italianate Earl of Oxford, who was an obvious mark for puritans. Lyly sided with Greene and Nashe against the Ramistic Harvey. Sidney's secretary was a Ramist – Sir William Temple. Oxford's secretary was the patrist old style Lyly."[15]

This was a *battle royale*. It was the old forces of medieval rhetoric against the new forces of plain speaking. It was the old rhetoric – which could not be penetrated, which mystified us while dancing before our eyes, which hypnotized us, tantalized us and frightened us, and was as holy as God's word, set dead against a new rhetoric – a rhetoric wary of decoration, and focused on succinct message, unembellished by unnecessary "ornamentation."

Sidney wrote *The Defense of Poesy* in 1579, defending poetry against puritan onslaughts; but he did so by claiming that art could be more puritanical than puritans themselves: "Therefore compare we the poet with the historian and with the moral philosopher; and if he go beyond them both, no other human skill can match him."[16] Like McLuhan, Mark Anderson clearly sees how the rhetorical battle lines were drawn. Anderson mentions that Sidney criticized art which – dangerously – demands too much of our imagination:

One theatrical innovation that Sidney strenuously objects to is the compression of time and space itself – condensing the scope of entire lives into a two-hour play, or continually shifting moods and setting without explaining each step to the audience [...] Now you have three ladies walk to gather flowers, and then we must believe the stage to be a garden. By and by, we hear news of shipwreck in the same place, then we are to blame if we accept it not for a rock ...While in the meantime two armies fly in represented with four shields and bucklers, and then what hard heart will not receive it for a pitched field?[17]

Anderson suggests that this speech by the *Henry V* chorus is Shakespeare's answer to Sidney – in direct opposition:

And so our scene must to the battle fly;
Where - O for pity! We shall much disgrace
With four or five most vile and ragged foils
Right ill disposed in brawl ridiculous
The name of Agincourt[18]

The rhetorical battle lines had been drawn. It was a cultural battle, one that moved far beyond Shakespeare, de Vere, Sidney and a disagreement in a tennis court. It would change the way we think and learn about the world. Much was gained, but also much was lost. Shakespeare is a door to the past; one that teases, tempts, and frustrates us – and perhaps may make us a little lonely and sad for a time long gone. But it is a door that must be opened.

Notes

[1]Jonson, Ben. "To the Memory of My Beloved the Author, Mr. William Shakespeare and What He Hath Left Us, Prefixed to the First Folio Edition of Shakespeare's Plays" https://www.bartleby.com/40/163.html. line 31 accessed March 31, 2019

[2]Hobbes, Thomas. *Leviathan.* https://www.gutenberg.org/files/3207/3207-h/3207-h. htm part 1 – Of Man. xiii accessed April 1, 2019

[3]Candido, Joseph. "The History of Shakespeare and Shakespeare in the Histories." Desai, R.W. (ed.) *Shakespeare the Man.* Fairleigh Dickinson University Press, 2014. 18

[4]White, R.S.. "1592-1594 Shakespeare's 'Other' Lost Years." Desai, R.W. (ed.) Shakespeare the Man. Fairleigh Dickinson University Press, 2014. 52

[5]Eliot, T.S. *The Sacred Wood and Major Early Essays*, Courier Corporation, 1997. 57

[6]Ibid., 58

[7]Ibid., 59

[8]Jonson, Ben. "On the Portrait of Shakespeare. https://www.bartleby.com/297/230. html lines 9-10, accessed March 31, 2019

[9]Hazlitt, William. "On Shakespeare and Milton." https://www.wwnorton.com/college/english/nael/noa/pdf/27636_Roma_U11_Hazlitt.pdf, accessed April 2, 2019

[10]Bloom, Harold. *Shakespeare: The Invention of the Human.* Riverhead Books, 1998. 14

[11]Ibid., 8

[12]*Hamlet.* (Folger, 2012) 3.1.167

[13]*A Midsummer Night's Dream.* (The RSC Shakespeare, 2008) 5.1.6

[14]Anderson, Mark. *Shakespeare by Another Name.* Gotham, 2005. 139

[15]McLuhan, Marshall. *The Classical Trivium.* Gingko Press, 2006. 210

[16]Sidney, Philip. "An Apology for Poetry" Morley, Henry. *Shorter works in English Prose: Cassel's Library of English Literature Vol 4.* Cassell, Petter & Galpin N.D., 1890-1900. 74

[17]Anderson, Mark. *Shakespeare by Another Name.* Gotham, 2005. 150

[18]*Henry V.* (Folger 1995) 4. P. 49-53

CHAPTER THREE

Grammar

Marshall McLuhan's doctoral thesis (*The Classical Trivium*, 1943) is a study of the early modern Harvey/Nashe literary controversy. Gabriel Harvey (and his brother Richard) competed with Thomas Nashe in a series of duelling pamphlets during the early 1590s. These pamphlets are terribly difficult for us to read now, as they were written with the variant spelling and dense syntax of the time, by two men deeply immersed in the rhetorical strategies of their day. The pamphlets are so difficult to decipher that pre-McLuhan scholars had no hope of moving beyond simply decoding them. The quarrel had a religious animus, but was not entirely religious in nature.

In 1583 John Whitgift, the Archbishop of Canterbury, took a tough stance; imprisoning puritans, confiscating their property, even executing them. The puritans fought back with the "Martin Marprelate" pamphlets named for the pseudonym of their author. In response, Whitgift hired several men to write against the puritans, including John Lyly, Robert Greene and Thomas Nashe. The Harveys became involved when they began answering the pamphlets of Nashe and Greene.

Examining the dynamics of an early modern literary quarrel might seem a far cry from McLuhan's later obsession with 20th century technology in *Understanding Media*. But *The Classical Trivium* is very much an examination of the effects of technological change. McLuhan's thesis is that Harvey and Nashe were arguing about how best to understand and perceive the world when the primary source of communication was in the process of relocating from the beauty and obscurity of human poetic invention, to the exacting, readily available, and eminently provable information provided in the pages of printed books devoted to the scientific method.

The classical trivium of McLuhan's title refers to the organization of medieval and early modern education. It focused on three subjects: grammar, dialectics and rhetoric. Rhetoric, in turn was divided into five parts: inventio (discovery), dispositio (arrangement), memoria (memory), elocutio (style) and pronunciatio (delivery). Many of these words did not mean what they mean today. Memory, for instance, referred not just to memorization but to the vast mechanism of our imagination as a whole. Grammar referred not simply to syntax, but to a way of perceiving the world. McLuhan sums up the cultural war between the modern period and the ancients as a quarrel between dialecticians and grammarians. He says: "From the point of view of the medieval grammarian, the dialectician was a barbarian." McLuhan proposes that today we live in an age when "dialectics" has triumphed.

Grammar is the most important of the three elements of the classical trivium to understand, because it is most alien to us. Though modern learning still contains the remnants of classical rhetoric, and dialectic has morphed into what we now know as logic and science, there is no equivalent today for the "grammar" – as it was used by medievals and early moderns.

Dialectics was – to the ancients – questions and answers in search of truth. McLuhan quotes Aristotle in his Topics: "It is through the opinions generally held on the particular points that these have to be discussed and this task belongs properly or most appropriately to dialectic: for dialectic is a process of criticism wherein lies the path to the principles of all inquiries."[1] During the Greek period, dialectics was mainly used to discuss politics and ethics; in the middle ages it was used to debate scripture. With Francis Bacon and Ramus in the 16th century dialectics became associated with what we now call the scientific method.

Rhetoric is best defined by the famous Roman rhetorician Cicero as eloquence, which, as McLuhan explains "implies wisdom, is a principal means by which the integrity of our nature is achieved once more, for eloquence operates on the passions of men via the imagination, controlling men for a common social good."[2] One of the fundamentals of a rhetorical education was the insistence that fine speech was the characteristic of a virtuous man. This is related to the relationship between grammar and rhetoric, for if language was beautiful, holy, and held secrets, then the oral enunciation of such language was guaranteed to not only help reveal the sacred knowledge to be found in words, but to enhance it.

Grammar and dialectic were opposing ways of understanding the world. For most of the medieval period, grammarians ruled. During the early modern period, grammarians were gasping their last, dying breaths. In my opinion, the last, and greatest gatekeeper of grammarian pedagogy was William Shakespeare.

It's difficult to define exactly what an education in early modern grammar was, simply because there is no equivalent today. The key is epistemology, which is how we come to understand the world and name things. Today we learn to perceive and categorize the world through our senses. This may sound elementary, but it was not elementary during the medieval period. "Through our senses" means that we observe the world, through taste, touch, sight, sound and smell. We then decide what things are. Then we name them.

This process has to do with comparing one thing to another. It also involves experimentation. We know for instance that water, when heated, appears to turn to vapour, and when cooled, appears to turn to solid. Is it still water? A more modern experimentation process would have us examine the molecules and see if they are the same. This kind of observation, experimentation, and logic is the epistemological process that utilizes the method that would have been called dialectics in the late 17th and early 18th centuries.

The use of the senses in Shakespeare's writing lies in direct opposition to this. Shakespeare's poetry is sensual, but related to synaesthesia. These means that Shakespeare – instead of utilizing the senses in scientific fashion to perceive the world, encourages us through metaphor to mix up the senses – and our perceptions. Synaesthesia is a neurological condition in which people find their senses are connected. For instance, a synaesthete might see colours when they hear musical notes.

A synaesthete, according to modern science, is perceiving *incorrectly* (i.e. is a "neural abnormal"), because music is not colour. But Shakespeare often confuses modes of perception. Bottom comically confuses the senses in a speech when he attempts to describe the experience of his dream: "The eye of man hath not heard, the ear of man hath not seen, man's hand is not able to taste, his tongue to conceive, nor his heart to report what my dream was. I will get Peter Quince to write a ballad of this dream. It shall be called 'Bottom's Dream' because it hath no bottom."[3]

This is not the only passage in which Shakespeare "mixes the senses" in what appears to be a critique of traditional perception. For instance, in *Love's Labour's Lost* Boyet says of the lovesick Navarre that his confession of love is spoken through his eyes: "I have only made a mouth of his eye / By adding a tongue which I know will not lie."[4]

It is significant also that Bottom suggests that the way to understand his dream might be to listen to music; because it is essentially unexplainable in words, and requires something more and less than logic. Bottom's wordplay on his own name is also significant. As Ron Rosenbaum points out in *The Shakespeare Wars*, Shakespeare was fond of the concept of "bottomlessness" utilizing it not only in his wordplay on "bottom" in *A Midsummer Night's Dream* but in other plays as well. Rosenbaum sees this as Shakespeare signalling to audiences that poetry offers unfathomable depths. He muses, ironically: "Was Shakespeare only thinking of weaver's spools and butts in naming one of his greatest characters bottom? Or is there an allusion as well to the deepest most bottomless mysteries of creation, the bottom of God's secrets?"[5]

Certainly bottomlessness is found everywhere in Shakespeare. Rosalind says to Celia in *As You Like It*: "Thou didst know how many fathom deep I am in love. But it cannot be sounded; my affection hath an unknown bottom, like the Bay of Portugal."[6] Shakespeare, like Hamlet ("more than is dreamt of in your philosophy"), seems to be assuring us that there is more in this world than can be understood through the logical use of our senses.

Some have argued that Shakespeare's use of metaphor is in itself synaesthetic and involves confusing normal perception. A. Cook's *Shakespearean Neuroplay* quotes a study in which synaesthesia and metaphor are called equivalents: "We can think of metaphors as involving cross activation of conceptual maps in synaesthesia."[7] When poets call agony a "horse" or love an "ocean," they are confusing our senses in order to make us understand something complex and profound.

Scholars have also found that metaphors are essential to the process of learning. As Raphael Lyne points out in *Shakespeare, Rhetoric and Cognition*, certain Shakespearean monologues are "processes of thought."[8] We often think in metaphor, by comparing something to something else. And often we use this technique – as Shakespeare's characters do – to try and understand things which cannot be explained easily.

Realizing that metaphors are an illogical and sensually confused way of understanding complex concepts perhaps provides a window into what the medieval study of grammar entailed. The principle – which may sound quite improbable to us now – is that the best way to perceive the world is to listen to, or read, a poem. The reality of the world is not to be found through our eyes, but through language. McLuhan explains the early modern concept of the subject of grammar like this:

> [L]anguage was viewed as simultaneously linking and harmonizing all the intellectual and physical functions of man and of the physical world as well ... the whole of nature was a book which he [Adam] could read with ease. He lost his ability to read this language of nature as a result of the fall ... The business of art is however, to recover the knowledge that language which once man held by nature.[9]

After Adam's fall, sacred books were required for learning. Before that, we could simply see the truth in nature; the sacred names of plants, stones and birds were revealed to us magically. After the fall, we lost that ability to read nature and the only way to discover it again was through poetry. McLuhan paraphrases Salutati from the 14th century:

> [W]e must study poetry because scripture employs the modes of poetry. Since we can have no concept of God, we can have no words in which to speak to him or of him, we must, therefore fashion a language based on his works. Only the most excellent mode will do, and this is poetry. Thus poetry may be outwardly false bur essentially true. Holy writ is of this kind. The origins of poetry are the foundations of the world.[10]

More recently in *The Order of Things* Foucault tries to articulate much the same concept. He speaks almost elegiacally of what was lost by the decline of a grammarian education:

> [T]he theory of representation disappears as the universal foundation of all possible orders; language as the spontaneous tabula, the primary grid of things, as an indispensable link between representation and things, is eclipsed ... above all, language loses its privileged position and becomes, in its turn, a historical form coherent with the density of its own past. But as things become increasingly reflexive, seeking the principle of their intelligibility only in their own development, and abandoning the space of representation, man enters in his turn, and for the first time, the field of Western knowledge.[11]

Thinking about the way metaphors work (and reading Foucault's and McLuhan's definitions of grammar) is as close as we may get to understanding the ancient discipline of grammar. Our comprehension of the subject will necessarily be inexact, because the study of grammar itself was inexact. McLuhan recognizes not only the limits of his own analysis but our modern inability to comprehend medieval grammar as a discipline: "We inevitably are attempting to deal with the complex and sophisticated intellectual disciplines provided by the trivium in the terms of the naïve literary and linguistic culture of our own day."[12]

The relation between grammar and the Harvey/Nashe conflict is complicated, as is the history of the classical trivium in general. Grammar, rhetoric and dialectics were hotly debated by scholars from their beginnings in ancient Greece. Which was the best discipline? The debate thrived through the medieval period and the early modern period – until the seismic shift that took place after the Renaissance.

The battle between medieval and early modern dialecticians and rhetoricians originated with the Greek debates between Stoics and the Sophists. Sophists argued and speechified – not with the primary purpose of establishing the truth – but to persuade the audience of their point of view through the beauty, abundance, elegance, and embellishment of language. The Sophists were masters of persuasion. Aristotle and Plato both wrote against the Sophists, because sophism was thought to be potentially dangerous. Stoics, on the other hand, claimed to speak only the unadorned truth, stripped of persuasion.

During the middle ages grammar and rhetoric were nurtured and protected by the church fathers' "patristic" teachings. Dialectics occasionally claimed victory over the other two elements of the trivium, until the humanist/grammarian celebration of language came to dominate western culture in the Renaissance – represented by writers such as Petrarch, Erasmus, and Shakespeare. The ancient polarization between Stoics and Sophists came to final fruition in the pamphlet war between the dialectical Harvey and grammatical/rhetorical Nashe. As McLuhan tells us:

> With the decadence of dialectical or scholastic theology in the fourteenth and fifteenth centuries both grammarians and rhetoricians surge forward again, finally triumphing in the work and influence of Erasmus, the restorer of patristic theology and of the grammatical humanistic discipline on which it rests. On the other hand, the war between the dialecticians and rhetoricians began as soon as the Sophists attempted to make dialectics subordinate to the art of persuasion. Plato and Aristotle were the greatest enemies of rhetoricians, not so much in rejecting rhetoric, as in asserting that as an art it had no power to control dialectics. The Stoics, however, are the main defenders of dialectics against rhetoric after Aristotle.[13]

Perhaps one of the reasons we now find the Harvey/Nashe quarrels so opaque is because the Harvey/Nashe pamphleteers took everyone's understanding of this issue for granted. McLuhan suggests that the language debate was culturally significant enough to make an appearance in Marlowe's *Dr. Faustus*. The play mentions Faust's passion to "live and die in Aristotle's works / Sweet Analytics, 'tis thou has ravished me! / ... Is to dispute well logic's chiefest end?"[14] Faust even picks up Jerome's Bible – recently translated by Erasmus – and tries to perform dialectical exegesis upon it. In other words, Dr. Faustus' tragic, over-reaching intellect was associated with dialectics, which early modern audience members would understand was very much under attack by Erasmus and humanism.

If one attempts to read the Harvey/Nashe pamphlets with their different attitudes to rhetoric in mind, one is immediately struck by how similar their styles seem to be. One might expect that a Stoic and a Sophist would not sound very much alike. They are not that different to *our* ear because we live in a cultural dominated not by orality, ancient grammar, and rhetoric, but by the printed book and the scientific method. Not everyone in the early modern period was effectively a rhetorician. But everyone who went to school learned to approach the world through the study of language and literature. In a culture that focuses on learning about the world through poetry, what might have been considered the simplest of rhetorical styles in their day seem complex to us.

So how do Harvey and Nashe manifest their differing views? Their debate centred around Petrus Ramus (1515-1572), a French philosopher whose work has been ignored somewhat because the content of his philosophy has proved less important than its historical effects. The general consensus is that Ramus did not have the depth of insight offered by his near contemporaries Descartes or Hobbes. But his ideas – though some of them may seem ill-conceived and even irrelevant today – changed the course of western history.

Technically, Ramus was a rhetorician like all learned men of his time. He was a student of Sturm, whom Edward De Vere visited in Germany. Sturm's pedagogical innovations (he invented the educational institution called the gymnasium) were instituted in Strassburg, Germany (now Strasbourg, France) – only 200 miles from Wittenberg, where Hamlet went to school. Though it's possible to see the connections between Sturm and Ramus, and also to understand what the younger man learned from his teacher, their attitudes to rhetoric were vastly different. Sturm was a humanist, obsessed with the Greek rhetorician Hermogenes. Though Ramus first gained notoriety for attacking Aristotle, scholars now agree that his scorn for the ancient Greeks lacked substance, and was mainly a self-serving strategy to gain attention; it seems more that Ramus attacked Aristotle because he wished to replace him. His revolutionary contribution to western history was to separate the five elements of rhetoric, thus weakening rhetoric and strengthening dialectics in the process.

Ramus moved inventio (discovery), dispositio (arrangement), memoria (memory) from rhetoric to dialectics, leaving rhetoric with only the elements of elocutio (style) and pronunciatio (delivery). His ideas became all the rage in the 17th century. There were many editions of his work, and even more importantly, his books were adopted as textbooks in graduate schools. Ramus' version of rhetoric is thus the rhetoric that we know today. Because Ramus castrated the ancient discipline, language no longer held the central place in the trivium. One of the most important aspects of rhetoric was memory, which really meant the imagination – our ability to store elaborate and stunning images, stories and words in our "mind's eye." Ramus, (as Ong informs us) was much indebted to the rhetorician Agricola, whose approach to language became analytic, meaning it was no longer the holy, mystical entity that grammarians and rhetoricians had once imagined:

> We ourselves think of books as "containing" chapters and para-
> graphs, paragraphs as "containing" sentences, sentences as "contain-
> ing" words, words as "containing" ideas, and finally ideas as "con-
> taining" truth. Here the whole mental world has gone hollow. The
> pre-Agricolan mind had preferred to think of books as saying some-
> thing, of sentences as expressing something, and of words and ideas
> as "containing" nothing at all, but rather as signifying or making
> signs for something.[15]

Now that the major elements of rhetoric were transferred to dialectic, speech and poetry could be denuded of the frippery which
hid the content. The job of dialectics was to see through the for-
est and find the trees, penetrate what Ramus considered to be
unnecessary verbiage, and – in stoical fashion – *find the truth*.
This stripping away of the "ceremonial robes" of language had
obvious religious implications. Puritans were dedicated to removing the fancy words, rituals, and costumes, of the church service
and instead allowing the common man direct access to the word
of god. In this cause, puritans called for Ramistic sermons, which
featured less verbal decoration and could be whittled down to
easily grasped simple statements that were morally unambiguous.

Harvey's book *Rameidos* praised Ramus. Harvey, Spenser and
Sidney formed a group called Areopagus. One of the poems to
emerge from this group, called *Speculum Toscanismi*, made fun
of Edward de Vere. When Edward de Vere learned of the poem,
Harvey denied it was about him. The poem made fun of de Vere's
effete Italianism. After de Vere returned from Italy he preferred
dressing in the Italian fashion, but of course, "Italianism" also is
a reference to the Renaissance humanist writers like Petrarch.

Significantly, Harvey's criticism of Oxford in his 1578
speech suggests that de Vere cease his "writings that serve no useful purpose." This is a recommendation directly based on Harvey's Ramism. For Ramus, the best language was useful – that is
clear, understandable, and with an unadulterated moral purpose.

Appearing in the same year as his speech delivered to Oxford was Harvey's play *Pedantius*. The play was apparently based on Oxford's offence at the manner in which he was represented in the satire *Speculum Toscanismi*. The play depicted a Ciceronian schoolmaster – i.e. a schoolmaster steeped in the ancient grammarian, humanistic rhetoric.

It seems likely that if de Vere *was* Shakespeare, then this would suggest Shakespeare was in the anti-Harvey, Nashe camp – hence the quarrel with Sidney, which McLuhan thinks was the basis of the whole Harvey/Nashe quarrel. But it's best to turn to Shakespeare's work for proof positive of his predilections.

Love's Labour's Lost, like all of Shakespeare's plays, is a play about language, but unlike some of his other plays, it is obviously and evidently concerned with words. This means that *Love's Labour's Lost* is difficult to read today, as it puts quite a "feast" of different styles before us. Today, that feast quite often confuses as much as it amuses.

Scholars, when placing the play in the context of the Harvey/Nashe controversy, try to identify certain characters in the play as Nashe, Harvey, or Sidney. The contrast in real life between Harvey and Nashe was between a university professor – a very learned and respected man – versus a man who positioned himself as an anarchic voice of immediacy. Nashe's criticism of Ramus angered Harvey. Nashe was a kind of fly in the ointment, buzzing in the ear of a stoical, puritanical academic.

It's therefore not particularly surprising that scholars should have seen a resemblance between Nashe and the character in *Love's Labour's Lost* who is sometimes called "Moth" and sometimes called "Boy" in various versions of the script. Moth is described as a "tender juvenal" and Nashe was referred to as a "juvenal" by Shakespeare's contemporaries Robert Greene and Francis Meres. Moth in the play is the attendant on Armado, who is a Spanish boaster. Armado's language is suitably over-blown. His comically pretentious phrasings are only matched by the pedant Holofernes (who some scholars have seen as a satire of Harvey).

Whether or not Holofernes is meant specifically to be Harvey, the satire of Holofernes in *Love's Labour's Lost* is a critique of a "scholastic" person. Scholasticism refers to the pedagogy which centred around rhetoric. Harvey, a teacher involved in the dense arguments about rhetorical figures and word usage, made scholastics ripe for satire. The pretensions of scholastic argument dominate this passage in which Armado and Holofernes argue over the word "afternoon":

> Armado. Sir, it is the kings most serious pleasure and affection to congratulate the princess at her pavilion in the posteriors of the day, which the rude multitude call the afternoon.
> Holofernes. The posterior of the day most generous sir, is liable con-gruent and measurable for the afternoon The word is well culled, chose, sweet and apt, I do assure you sir, I do assure.[16]

Moth, the deflator of pretension – who uses language in a much more casual and irreverent way – pokes fun at them: "They have been at a great feast of languages, and stolen the scraps."[17]

In order to further make connections between the Harvey/Nashe controversy and *Love's Labour's Lost*, scholars also search for direct references to it in the play. For instance, Holofernes' devoted acolyte Nathaniel says of him: "Sir I praise the Lord for you and so are the parishioners … [whose] daughters profit very greatly under you."[18] This is only the second time Shakespeare uses the word "parishioners" in all his works (the other reference in *As You Like it*, which is also thought to be a reference to Harvey in the character of Oliver Martext – a drunken priest). The reference to Harvey comes because he was accused of giving his women parishioners "holy kisses." Also, as Francis Yates notes, Shakespeare has clearly borrowed the obscure joke about "piercing a hogshead"[19] in *Love's Labour's Lost* from Harvey's *Pierces Supererogation*.

This kind of debate is easy to get lost in, and almost impossible to resolve. I would contend that none of Shakespeare's characters were modelled after a single person. Like most authors, Shakespeare writes characters that are conglomerates of many, including perhaps himself. So let's examine what *Love's Labour's Lost* is actually *about*. In *Love's Labour's Lost* Shakespeare expresses a very particular and complex rhetorical point of view, grounded in the complex rhetorical controversies of his time.

The play has hardly any plot at all. Three young men travel to study with the King of Navarre. They promise to forgo love for study, dedicating themselves to an ascetic existence devoid of human pleasure, for a period of three years. As soon as they agree on this pact, three beautiful young women arrive with the Princess of France. The men spend the rest of the play breaking their promise, perjuring themselves; "lying" because they all fall in love. The bulk of the play is concerned with the women exposing the men's hypocrisy, and to discussions about the proper focus of pedagogy. Should our "study" be focused on books, or can we – should we – learn from love and beauty?

Love's Labour's Lost was most likely written by a young man with an extensive early modern education. Students typically finished graduate school at age 18 – many went directly into teaching. So young Shakespeare would have been fresh from participating in the rhetorical debates of the time, and deeply concerned with issues of rhetoric, language, and truth. On the surface of it, the play seems to be ridiculing traditional education and rhetoric. But one of the problems with this interpretation is that *Love's Labour's Lost* is *itself* "poetic" – in other words it utilizes the figures and

tropes of poetry and prose – i.e. rhetoric – in abundance, sometimes to great persuasive effect, especially in the lengthy speeches
of the leading character Berowne.

This is the fundamental paradox in Shakespeare's work. He is
always critical of language and its uses; but the contradiction of
course is that he *uses language to write about language*. In fact the
only medium that he has (or any of us has) to critique language,
is language itself. And more than that – Shakespeare's rhetorical
technique is not ultimately "Ramist." Though he critiques language he rarely himself uses language which is stripped of figures
or metaphors. He does quite the opposite in all of his writing; he
piles metaphor upon metaphor.

It is as if Shakespeare is waving to us from the glorious shipwreck that is language, poetry, metaphor, and rhetorical figure,
trying to make us understand what he is saying. Or is he? For
he refuses to use anything other than the most sophisticated and
complex, indeed most bewitching metaphors to express his ideas.
Thus his critique of language is simultaneously completely evident – and completely obscured. Shakespeare was certainly conscious of this labyrinthine contradiction. In fact, it is the most
significant paradox of perception that he wishes to present to us.
All we have is language; but language is dangerously unreliable;
so, paradoxically, let's utilize all of the magic of language to speak
about how untrustworthy language itself is.

Love's Labour's Lost is obsessed with the polysemous nature
of language; the fact that words may mean more than one thing,
and often do. Simple communication is often compromised. The
conversations of the scholastics/boasters – Holofernes, Nathaniel and Armado – often misfire as they are centred on puns with
more than one meaning (some of which are incomprehensible to
us because they reference early modern songs, legends and sayings
that are obscure today). But some puns are still persuasively clear.

For instance, Moth assures Armado that his escape will be as "swift as lead."[20] Armado is confused because lead is a heavy, hard metal. Or is it? Moth explains: "Is that lead slow which is fired from a gun?"[21]

Similarly, when Dumain speaks of his love for Kate, he says that she is a "fever in his blood" and Berowne corrects him: "A fever in your blood! why, then incision / Would let her out in saucers: sweet misprision!"[22] Berowne is saying that if Kate is a "fever in his blood" then all Dumain must do to rid himself of her is bleed himself (one of the trusted cures of the day). Dumain's love for Kate would thus end up in a saucer. Berowne observes that this idea is a lovely and quite apt misunderstanding, because of course it is a sign of the intensity of Dumain's feelings that he cannot rid himself of his passion by bleeding. It would be the same as saying to someone who is in love: "Have your blood pressure checked – that'll cure it!" Misprision was a legal term for "the deliberate concealment of one's knowledge of a treasonable act or a felony." The misprision is "sweet" because it says so many things at once, and thus takes full advantage of the polysemous nature of language.

If the young men in *Love's Labour's Lost* have come to Navarre to study, one would assume that they have come to study rhetoric, the much debated primary philosophical obsession of the time under scholastics like Holofernes. Obstructing them are two obstacles – the beauty of the women, and the idiocy of the pedants and boasters at court. By the end of act four, Berowne has "graduated" to the conclusion that books are not the source of wisdom – love is. But Berowne's critique of rhetoric is not a rejection of poetry or a rejection of the grammarian approach to perception. On the contrary, it is a confirmation of the importance of poetry and grammar. It is a rejection of quarrelling, boasting scholastics, bad pedagogy, and Ramist dialectics that were beginning to dominate education at the time.

Berowne comes to believe that the only way to understand the world is not through our senses, but through love: "A lover's eye will gaze an eagle blind. / A lover's ear will hear the lowest sound, / When the suspicious head of theft is stopped. / Love's feeling is more swift and sensible than are the tender horns of cocked snails."[23] Ramus' new dialectics demanded people understand the world by directly examining it with their five senses and clearly expressing the truth found there. Instead, Berowne, would have us understand the world by looking into his beloved Rosaline's eyes. And what is love for Berowne? It is synonymous with poetry: "Subtle as the sphinx, as sweet and musical / As bright Apollo's lute strung with his hair."[24]

Berowne's attack on Boyet reveals more about his anti-Ramist attitude. Boyet is the chaperone of the beautiful young women. (Some scholars suggest Sidney was the inspiration for the character.) More importantly, Berowne's criticism of Boyet is interesting because he berates him for doing exactly what Harvey asks de Vere to do in his famous speech: i.e. make language useful: "This fellow pecks up wit as pigeons peas / And utters it again when God doth please / He is wits peddler and retails his wares / At wakes and wassails, meetings, markets, fairs. / And we that sell by gross the lord doth know / Hath not the grace to grace it with such show."[25] Berowne here is clearly contrasting the denotative, useful language of the marketplace with poetry which is impractical, resonant, allusive, even holy.

Berowne's conflation of poetry and love is neoplatonic in origin. Neoplatonism was a branch of Christianity influenced by Plato, that flourished during the Middle Ages under the patristic philosophers. It was a a major influence on early modern humanists. Neoplatonists sought to incorporate Greek and Roman philosophy into Christianity. As John Vyvyan tells us, according to neoplatonism "the soul is born to do a definite work – to reshape the world into the likeness of heaven; that it already possesses the heavenly pattern in its own self-nature ... concealed by the physical form; and that it will only be re-discovered by the insight of true love."[26]

Neoplatonism was a likely sister philosophy to grammarian teaching; for both understood beauty and poetry to be reflections of the world's truth. For Berowne, love is music "when love speaks, the voice of all the gods make heaven drowsy with the harmony."[27] This reverence for poetry, harmony and beauty is what Berowne has in common with Nashe, who here – in his criticism of Harvey – contrasts the barrenness of Ramist rhetoric with the profundity of poetry:

> These Bussards think knowledge a burthen ...They contemns Arts as unprofitable, contenting themselves with a little Country Grammar knowledge ... I account of Poetrie, as of a more hidden and divine kind of Philosophy, enwrapped in blind Fables and dark stories, wherein the principles of more excellent Arts and morals precepts of manners illustrated with divers examples of other Kingdoms and Countries are contained ... in Poems, the things that are most profitable are shrouded under Fables that are most obscure.[28]

Nashe's grammarian approach to rhetoric is akin to Berowne's equation of love, poetry and music as modes of perception.

In contrast to poetry, Berowne says: "Other slow arts entirely keep the brain / And therefore, finding barren practitioners, / Scarce show a harvest of their heavy toil."[29] Berowne is clearly referring to dialectics and the newly burgeoning early sciences, like astronomy. When Berowne criticizes traditional learning at the beginning of the play, he directly attacks the "art" of astronomy, dismissing "Those earthly godfathers of heavens lights / That give a fixed name to every star / Have no more profit of their shining nights / Than those that walk and wot not what they are. Too much to know is to know naught but fame; / And every godfather can give a name."[30]

Berowne also shares this attitude with Nashe. Nashe speaks of astronomers with scorn saying they "dreamed strange devises of the sunne and moon and they like gipsies wandring up and down told fortunes, juggled nicknamed all the starres, and were of idiots termed philosophers."[31]

But Berowne's crusade to reject Ramist dialectics – and to replace it with the poetry of love – is not the final revelation of the play. *Love's Labour's Lost* goes a step further.

Though Berowne speaks beautifully of love and poetry, the object of his poetic appeals – Rosaline – is critical of the ornate, sophistic language he uses to describe her. She criticizes him for the pretension of peppering his love poetry with French words:

> Berowne: My love to thee is sound, sans crack or flaw
> Rosaline: Sans "sans" I pray you
> Berowne: Yet I have a trick
> of the old rage, Bear with me, I am sick; I'll leave it by degrees[32]

After the entertainment in Act Five, Marcade enters to announce that the father of the Princess of France has died. Rosaline chides Berowne's language again, and he seems suddenly ashamed of his poetical words and obsession with beauty. He effectively turns into a Ramist, as death makes poetry impossible: "Honest plain words best pierce the ear of grief."[33]

But he is not a Ramist for long. Rosaline's final demand of Berowne is not that he abandon rhetoric. He just needs a *better* rhetoric. And what would that be? Go visit a hospital, she says, and: "converse with groaning wretches; and your task shall be, with all the fierce endeavour of your wit, to enforce the pained impotent to smile."[34] Notice that she does not demand that Berowne preach dry moralism to the dying – as puritans would have it – or tell them the unvarnished truth as Ramus and other Stoics would require. Instead he should use his "wit" to make them "smile." Berowne is not sure if that is possible, but she says: "A jest's prosperity lies in the ear / Of him that hears it, never in the tongue / Of him that makes it."[35] It is not enough for Berowne to say what he thinks charming by his own standard – the words must communicate to the hearer.

What are we to make of this?

Shakespeare gives us one clue. At the end of the play there are two songs: one sung by spring, and then another sung by winter. Spring is the season of love, and winter of death.

The imagery used by spring, ("Ver") is lighter and more picturesque, cheerier, less gritty. There is a mention of the subject of so many comedies – adultery, but in a mild and metaphorical way, not even as cuckoldry, but as a cuckoo bird: "The cuckoo then on every tree / Mocks married men, for thus sings he."[36]

In contrast, the vision of Winter ("Heim") is bleaker and of course colder, and somewhat, well, more carnal, with two references to "greasy Joan," one of them here: "While greasy Joan doth keel the pot./ When all aloud the wind doth blow, /And coughing drowns the parson's saw."[37] After these songs are sung, Armado says: "The words of Mercury are harsh after the songs of Apollo. You that way; we this way."[38] These are the last words of the play.

Some scholars think Armado is merely directing the characters where to walk. At the very least, we can be sure that Shakespeare ended Love's Labour's Lost with a paradoxical riddle. And the implication is that some people will take one road (believe one thing) and some people will take another (believe something else).

What do these two choices represent? What would Shakespeare and his audience have considered to be the difference between Apollo and Mercury? Ben Jonson in his famous poem "To the Memory of My Beloved the Author, Mr. William Shakespeare" says: "When, like Apollo, he came forth to warm / Our ears, or, like a Mercury, to charme."[39] What is the difference between "warming" and "charming"? Leslie Hotson made a study of Mercury and Apollo in an early modern context in *Shakespeare by Hilliard*. Hotson contends that Hilliard's famous miniature painting of a hand reaching from a cloud to touch the hand of a young man is meant to be a portrait of the God Apollo reaching from the clouds to touch the hand of Shakespeare/Mercury. Certainly eloquent "honey-tongued" poets of the early modern period were often associated with Mercury.

Apollo was the God of poetry, Mercury of eloquence. What is the difference between poetry and eloquence? Legend has it that Mercury stole Apollo's oxen, making the God angry. Mercury then gave Apollo his lyre, and the two of them made beautiful music together. Does this mean poetry and eloquence are the same? No. Apollo is unquestionably one of the greatest of Gods, whereas Hermes, in contrast, is the God who most resembles humans. The difference between them in early modern eyes had a lot to do with their method of communication.

As Hotson tells us (quoting Littleton), Apollo was associated with oracles and messages which were riddling or "oblique." This means that he was prone to "speaking ambiguously, so that he may be taken divers ways."[40] Mercury, as the God of eloquence, represents something quite different; a voice that crosses boundaries and languages. Because he was often mistaken for a man, Mercury was like a bridge between the divine and the human. Also, very significantly, Hermes is a bridge to *communicating with anyone*, by *adapting what he says to the ear of any specific audience*.

Shakespeare's final explication of Rosaline's advice then, is that "wit" must be oblique and riddled, but also must speak to everyone in many different ways. One did not learn this kind of rhetoric in most early modern graduate schools, through endless scholastic argument about tropes and figures. Shakespeare's point of view is again much like Nashe's who (according to Francis Yates) "extols the superiority of the debtors' prison over the universities as a school of wit."[41]

Nashe was certainly in alliance with Mercury, and would wish to remind us – as Winter (Mercury) does at the end of *Love's Labour's Lost*, that "greasy Joan" is ever stirring the pot. In *Love's Labour's Lost*, Berowne criticizes Boyet because he is a man who "when he plays at tables, chides the dice / In honourable terms."[42] For Berowne, the poet's rhetorical enemy is a man who is too polite to swear.

Shakespeare's rhetorical vision is a paradoxical conflation of Apollonian riddling (the obscure holiness of the grammarian) – and Mercurial adaptability; words that speak to every person, no matter how great or small, how smart or stupid, good or evil, simple or complex. How can what is beautiful and complex also be what is simple and true? What kind of magical rhetoric is that?

The answer can be found in Shakespeare's teacher: Hermogenes.

Notes

[1]McLuhan, Marshall. *The Classical Trivium*. Gingko Press, 2006. 48

[2]Ibid., (187)

[3]*A Midsummer Night's Dream*. (The RSC Shakespeare, 2008) 4.1. 211-215

[4]*Love's Labour's Lost*. (Folger, 1996) 2.1. 266-267

[5]Rosenbaum, Ron. *The Shakespeare Wars*. Random House, 2008. 16

[6]*As You Like It* (Folger, 1997) 4.1. 220-221

[7]Cook, Amy. *Shakespearean Neuroplay*. Palgrave, Macmillan, 2010. 25

[8]Lyne, Raphael. *Shakespeare, Rhetoric and Cognition*. Cambridge University Press, 2011. 11

[9]McLuhan, Marshall, *The Classical Trivium*. Gingko Press, 2006. 16.

[10]Ibid., 158

[11]Foucault, Michel. *The Order of Things*. Routledge, 2005. xxv

[12]McLuhan, Marshall, *The Classical Trivium*. Gingko Press, 2006. 105

[13]Ibid., 42

[14]Marlowe, Christopher. *Dr. Faustus*. Manchester University Press, 1993. 1.1. 5-8

[15]Ong, Walter J. Ramus, *Method, and the Decay of Dialogue*. Harvard University Press, 1958. 121

[16]*Love's Labour's Lost*. (Folger 2009) 5.1. 87-94

[17]Ibid., 5.1. 38-39

[18]Ibid., 4.2. 90-93

[19]Ibid., 4.2 105

[20]Ibid., 3.1. 58

[21]Ibid., 3.1. 64

[22]Ibid., 4.3. 101-102

[23]Ibid., 4.3 328-332

[24]Ibid., 4.3 336-337

[25]Ibid., 5.2. 347-352

[26]Vyvyan, John. *Shakespeare and Platonic Beauty*. Chatto and Windus, 1961. 45

[27]*Love's Labour's Lost*. (Folger 2009) 4.3. 38-39

[28]Nashe, Thomas. "The Anatomy of Absurdity." *The Complete Works of Thomas Nashe Vol 1*. Huth Library 1883-84. lines 36-37

[29]*Love's Labour's Lost*. (Folger, 2009). 4.3. 18-20

[30]Ibid., 1.1. 90-95

[31]Nashe, Thomas, "Summer's Last Will and Testament." *The Complete Works of Thomas Nashe Vol 6*. Huth Library 1883-84. lines 1408-1411

[32]*Love's Labour's Lost* (Folger, 2009). 5.2. 453-455

[33]Ibid., 5.2. 828

[34]Ibid., 5.2. 922

[35]Ibid., 5.2. 934-936

[36]Ibid., 5.2. 981-982

[37]Ibid., 5.2. 993-995

[38]Ibid., 5.2. 1002-1003

[39]Jonson, Ben. "To the Memory of My Beloved the Author, Mr. William Shakespeare and What He Hath Left Us, Prefixed to the First Folio Edition of Shakespeare's Plays" https://www.bartleby.com/40/163.html. lines 45-46 accessed March 31, 2019

[40]Hotson, Leslie. *Shakespeare by Hilliard*. Chatto and Windus, 1997. 96

[41]Yates, Francis. *A Study of Love's Labour's Lost*. Cambridge, 1936. 74

[42]*Love's Labour's Lost* (Folger, 2009) 5.2. 368-369

CHAPTER FOUR

Hermogenes

Hermogenes is not to be confused with Socrates' philosopher friend of the same name. Hermogenes of Tarsus, the rhetorician, was only creative for a brief period; he tragically lost his faculties at age 25. Several books are attributed to him. But only two of those books – *On Stasis* and *On Types of Style* – are absolutely confirmed to be his. Hermogenes' works might have been unknown to us if not for the Byzantine philosopher George of Trebizond, who visited Italy in the 15th century and made Renaissance humanists aware of Hermogenes' work.

Lawrence Green tells us that when Renaissance writers were interested in the details of figures of rhetoric "they turned to Hermogenes."[1] Nevertheless Hermogenes' work has been misunderstood and even despised. Annabel Patterson points out that in the *Oxford Classical Dictionary* J.W.H. Atkins dismisses *On Types of Style* as "a treatise notable for its endless classifications, distinctions, definitions, and rules, which added but little to the vital appreciation of style … Thus in the second and later century did Greek rhetoric revert to sterile scholastic standards and methods. It gave rise to a system which had disastrous effects on literature for centuries to come."[2]

One appeal of *On Types of Style* is that it offers a system. This was attractive to 16th century teachers of rhetoric, and most importantly to their students, who were drowning in the endless and complex rhetorical analysis that was associated with scholasticism. Though Hermogenes divides style into 20 categories instead of the usual three associated with Cicero, his book is nevertheless nothing if not ripe for application. Green tells us that Sturm was a renowned expert on Hermogenes: "The Hermogenean credentials of Johan Sturm are impeccable, He produced Greek and Latin Editions of Hermogenes with commentaries in 1570 and 1571."[3] Harvey tells us – in his ode to De Vere – that the young nobleman visited Sturm on his journey to Europe in 1575. Does it make sense that Shakespeare would have been interested in a "style manual" that was popular in the early modern period?

Petrus Ramus certainly was. As a student of Sturm's, Ramus was part of a pedagogical movement aimed at a more pragmatic approach to education. Students responded positively to a university education that was useful – especially for their subsequent teaching. Scholars have suggested that it was Ramus' fondness for organizational methods and manuals that drew him to Sturm.

The fact that Hermogenes' *On Types of Style* has the superficial appearance of a style manual may explain its popularity with Ramus (and many others at the time). After all, the treatise begins with the assurance than anyone can be a great orator like Demosthenes if they work hard enough at the craft. But to suggest this had anything to do with Sturm's attraction to Hermogenes would not be true. *On Types of Style* is not *simply* a handy style guide.

For example, the title may have been a mistranslation. Walter Ong suggests that perhaps a more accurate translation from the Latin would be: "On the Method of Scoring Rhetorical Effectiveness." Or perhaps, he says, that is not completely accurate: "A current sense of the term method in English fails to convey the signification of the original cognate here, which means something more like mode of rhetorical organization through structure ... so that the title might more properly be rendered On the Pattern of Underlying Rhetorical Irresistibility."[4]

On Types of Style was thus intended as a philosophical treatise and was treated as such by Sturm and by other neoplatonists. Ong specifies that Hermogenes rejected philosophy and wanted to separate philosophy and rhetoric, because rhetoric was, in itself, a philosophy: "His whole work is dominated by the policy of leaving all explanation to the 'philosophers' and erecting what von Christ calls a 'wall of separation' between philosophy and his own field, rhetoric ... clearly rhetorical and a-logical."[5]

Sturm's interest in Hermogenes was as a rhetorician and a grammarian in the medieval sense. Annabel Patterson tells us that Sturm taught Hermogenes from a neoplatonic perspective: "Hermogenes was not only a rhetorician but also a philosopher, and a platonic philosopher at that, according to his own words."[6] Sturm's neoplatonic interpretation of Hermogenes was related to the notion that the "forms" of neoplatonic perfection are rarely if ever glimpsed by us in reality. When we do see the perfect forms of the soul they appear only sporadically in natural and human beauty, and in art.

As Patterson also tells us, Sturm taught that the "patterns of things may never be found in actuality among fallible human beings; and yet the existence of the Idea consoles both the artist who abstracted it and the audience who admire it for the normal imperfection in their lives."[7] Patterson likens Sturm's approach to Hermogenes to Tasso's attitude that poetry is divine: "God himself by whom we are created, is a poet, and the divine art, by which he made the world is as it were the art of poetry and his poem is the Heaven and the whole world to which highest and sweetest concord human ears are perhaps deaf and closed."[8] Green suggests that when Sturm taught Hermogenes he equated his different "styles" with "ideas" ("idea" is the platonic word for ideal form): "For an idea is nothing other than a kind of speaking which is both excellent and appropriate."[9]

Most Elizabethan poets were influenced by neoplatonism, but this does not mean they shared the same attitudes to language. De Vere and Sidney were both neoplatonists. However de Vere visited Sturm, while Sidney was quite excited by Ramus and made a concerted attempt to bring his rhetorical theories to England. The Shakespeare/Nashe camp and the Sidney/Harvey camp differed in terms of their attitude to meaning. The ancient grammarian way was to value words (form) more than their meaning (matter). McLuhan reminds us that the Elizabethan teacher Ascham opined "Ye know not, what ye do to learning, that care not for wordes, but for matter, and so make a deuorce betwixt the tong and the hart."[10]

For Ramus and Sidney poetic expression was potentially dangerous because it could cloak the all important moral message, the meaning. McLuhan reminds us that Gosson's anti-theatricalist attack on theatre – *Schoole of Abuse* (1579) – "is professedly a Ramist tract dedicated to a Ramist [Sidney]"[11] Unlike Sidney, Shakespeare was a poet of the theatre and the spoken word; cognizant not only that meanings shift and can be illusory, but that the slipperiness of meaning is perhaps the point of language. For Shakespeare the relationship between matter and form is primary; a vast number of Shakespeare's metaphors raise the paradoxical notion that the outside (face, body, clothing, ornament, words) often hides what is inside (the soul, the truth).

In *Hamlet*, for instance, relationship between form and content seems to be on Gertrude's mind when she orders Polonius, in Ramistic fashion, to cease his poetic digressions and get to the point: "More matter, with less art."[12] Here she clearly separates form and content in Ramistic manner. Hamlet, on the other hand, when he converses with Polonius, seems to be suggesting that words are nothing more than that, and that if they do have meaning, that meaning is useless and nonsensical:

Polonius. What do you read, my Lord?

Hamlet. Words, words words.

Polonius. What is the matter, my Lord?

Hamlet. Between who?

Polonius. I mean the matter that you read, my lord.

Hamlet. Slanders, sir; for the satirical rogue says here that old men have gray beards.[13]

Hamlet's answer is literal when Polonius asks him what he is reading; he says "words" – i.e. the form, not the content. Polonius finds this answer unsatisfying. When Polonius tries to get Hamlet to reveal the meaning behind the words, by asking what is the "matter," Hamlet misunderstands Polonius to be asking him about his emotional relationship with Ophelia. This is a pun, a "quibble," related to the polysemous nature of language. When Hamlet finally understands that he is being asked to explain what he is reading, he says that the book is lies ("slander"). But the quotation he gives as an example – "old men have grey beards" – is something we know, paradoxically, to be true.

It is important that the passage involves reading a book and interpreting it. It's likely that Hamlet holds a printed book. Printed books and handwritten books were very different technologies. P.K. Ayers suggests that it is important to note that handwritten books were quite often read aloud, not read in private. He also suggests that "when Polonius asks Hamlet what he reads the implication is that Hamlet is either reading silently or mumbling. The former seems more probable given his sophistication in related matters; if such is the case this suggest an orientation toward the new technology."[14]

Shakespeare does not seem to have been very interested in printed books. His plays were only available in often wildly inconsistent printed "quartos" during his lifetime – not in the larger more impressive "folio" form. This may be because at the dawn of the printing press, books were associated with manuals, diagrams, and "systems." As Ong tells us, the printing press brought "new ideas about how to arrange the spoken word in space ... [that] finally played out in the Ramist dichotomies and into the new post-Gutenberg quest of philosophical 'systems.'"[15]

Claudius and Gertrude mention Hamlet going to school in northern Wittenberg. Only a few miles away he would have studied under Sturm, in Strassburg. Hamlet's strange answers to Polonius' questions seem to point to a critique of Ramism, dialectical critique, and printed books.

But this is conjecture; if we wish to prove that Shakespeare was part of the Elizabethan anti-Ramist camp we need not scour Hamlet's conversation with Polonius for its subtext, nor need we relentlessly examine Hamlet's appearance reading a book. It is Shakespeare's stylistic technique that betrays his grammarian roots and anti-Ramist sentiments. For though the incomprehensibility of Hamlet's madness makes us suspicious of language the way Ramus did, Shakespeare's style is not characterized by a Ramistic leanness of form. Quite the opposite. Shakespeare's work not only incorporates the recommendations of *On Types of Style* – as quintessential style manual – it echoes the philosophical implications of Hermogenes' philosophical attitude to beauty and truth.

One of the most common rhetorical techniques utilized by Shakespeare is antithesis. It is difficult to find a page in a play by Shakespeare that does not contain it. Shakespeare seems compelled – when speaking of one thing – to also speak of its opposite. One thinks of Macbeth, where Macbeth's confrontation with his own evil nature is wrapped up with polarized opposites, such as "fair is foul and foul is fair,"[16] and "nothing is but what is not."[17] When confronted with the witches Banquo wonders "can the devil speak true?"[18] And when the witches disappear Macbeth is amazed because "what seemed corporal melted."[19]

The examples throughout Shakespeare's work are too numerous to mention. Shakespeare's most famous monologue is structured around antithesis: "To be or not to be – that is the question."[20] Of course antithesis is an ancient rhetorical technique. Aristotle used it as the foundation of his ancient theory of epistemology "A is A," that one thing cannot be another. It's origins go back – as Sloane tells us – to the very roots of rhetoric and dialectics:

> The old presocratic expression of contraries appears in Plato as a method of discussion (dialectic) and argument (telenchus). Aristotle, in fact, in the opening of *Rhetoric* calls rhetoric the counterpoint of dialectic … All of these forms of philosophical argumentation and proof involve a dualism either of content or structure … Aristotle finds such antithetical expression pleasant (hedeia) "because contraries are most easily understood and are even more comprehensible if they are balanced, and further because antithesis is like a syllogism; for the argument (elanchos) is a bringing together of antithetical pairs" (Rhetoric 3.9.1410a). The parallel between this philosophical track that antithesis directed and the evolution of the periodic structure of sophisticated prose, found specifically in the speeches of Demosthenes, is not lost on Aristotle.[21]

I quote this passage from the *Encyclopaedia of Rhetoric* at length to prove not only that antithesis is the basis of both dialectics and rhetoric, but because Sloane mentions that one of the greatest of all rhetoricians – Demosthenes (Hermogenes' ideal orator) – utilized antithesis. Castiglione's *Book of The Courtier* – the rhetorical manual for courtier poets – recommended the use of antithesis, and antithesis dominated euphuism, the popular early modern writing style associated with John Lyly.

Because rhetoric and dialectics have a very different relationship to truth, they also find different reasons for antithesis. In dialectics the purpose of antithesis – that is, argument – is to ferret out the truth. In rhetoric the purpose of antithesis is less obvious.

Certainly, it can be, as Aristotle suggests, "pleasant" and edifying. This is the difference between antithesis and paradox. Antithesis searches for an answer, and is not satisfied until one is found. Paradox – which exemplifies Shakespeare's use of antithesis – offers us an eternally unanswered question. This lack of resolution has resounding implications.

Paradox is a "Hermogenean" approach. Hermogenes' two most important books – *On Issues* and *On Types of Style* – are both significantly concerned with paradox. On Issues articulates what is probably the most thorough diaeretic analysis of argument that anyone has ever attempted; Hermogenes' ideas are still taught in law classes today. Monfasani informs us that for "Hermogenes of Tarsus, a firm knowledge of status was not merely a perquisite for initiation into the higher mysteries of stylistic forms, it was also practically equivalent to invention. The key which unlocked this gateway to rhetoric was diaeresis (division)."[22]

On Issues was concerned with invention (inventio) which is the first category of rhetoric and the basis for – well, *everything*. Inventio was one of the categories, along with dispositio, which was removed from rhetoric by Ramus; it became discovery, in the modern, scientific sense. "Inventio" answers the question – what are the things which we wish to think and talk about?

What do we think and talk about in the modern world? Mainly, the world as we know it through our senses. What did early moderns think and talk about? Some early modern humanists had commonplace books (Montaigne did) which were written lists, as Ong tells us, of "a mass of abstract truths, hair raising expressions, detached phrases, comparisons, whole sentences, syllogism, collections of adjectives – this "copie" could be exploited at all cognitive levels, sensory and intellectual simultaneously … This store is drawn on in rhetoric for 'amplification.'"[23]

One idea that distinguishes rhetoric from dialectics is the notion that we have to decide what is worth talking and thinking about, as opposed to automatically turning to the world around us as a source for discussion and thought.

So Hermogenes devoted an elaborate system of invention to discover what deserves our attention. This inevitably meant issues and occurrences. Conley says: "It is in his breakdown of stasis headings, however, that Hermogenes is usually held to have achieved unprecedented elegance, for there Hermogenes links the headings in an orderly progression of contrary predicates – clear/unclear, complete/incomplete, and others – in a way no earlier writer had done before."[24] Szakolczai calls Hermogenes' list of issues "exhaustive, potentially infinite series of dichotomies until all possible states were exhausted."[25]

Hermogenes *On Issues*, written originally as a guide to invention in rhetoric, would have offered the orator a virtual fountain of paradoxical notions about anything; and given him a variety of paradoxes to set against each other in any speech. Today it is used by lawyers in a more scientific and dialectical fashion, to come up with all the facts of an argument that must be considered in a courtroom. Remember, McLuhan tells us that that "the study of law and rhetoric were so closely associated that legal studies were usually subsumed under rhetorical studies… [and] legal rhetoric took a literary turn"[26] – which explains why this rhetorical treatise by Hermogenes has now become a legal one.

In contrast to *On Issues*, *On Types of Style* is a purely rhetorical document, in which the opposites cannot be used to "find the truth" – at leas not in a dialectical sense – but to create pleasant and appealing paradoxes that seduce and persuade the listener. Hermogenes' rhetorical innovation was to divide style into seven different sub-categories, which he then proceeded to divide even further. Ciceronian rhetoric had offered rhetoricians the simplicity of three styles: low, medium and high – either plain, pleasant, or persuasive. Hermogenes, in contrast, offered seven categories of style: clarity, grandeur, beauty, rapidity, character, sincerity, and finally "force" (deinotes). "Clarity" can be sub-divided into two categories: purity and distinctness. "Grandeur" can be sub-divided into six different categories: solemnity, asperity, brilliance, abundance, vehemence, and florescence. "Character" can be sub-divided into four categories: simplicity, sweetness, subtlety and modesty. And "sincerity" has one sub-category: indignation. Confused yet? You may very well be. But I would suggest that to a rhetorician with Shakespeare's skill and inclinations this detailed analysis would have been more than invaluable; it would have been a godsend.

When Hermogenes speaks of this final perfect style ("force"), he uses paradox to make his point about the challenges involved for the perfect orator:

> For how would it not be difficult to mix purity with abundance, clarity with what is excessive and full, or to mix the insignificant with the solemn, the graceful with the grand, the simple with the vehement, the pleasant with the harsh, beauty where audacity is needed, or the ornamental with the persuasive, or the concise and the argumentative, and what is everyday thought not cheap or base, with what is thrilling or the persuasive, and that which expressed truth and what comes from the heart with what is florescent, and whatever kinds of style with those that seem by nature to be their opposite … we shall wait until we discuss the approach that is characteristic of Force to illustrate this more clearly.[27]

Here Hermogenes suggests that the juxtaposition of opposite stylistic approaches is the key to "force." But he never gets around to explaining exactly how this feat might occur. I would suggest that Shakespeare's work is the realization of Hermogenes' promise.

Paradox is an essential element of Hermogenes' classifications.

When explaining the various styles, Hermogenes often contrasts them as opposites. He suggests that "abundance" is the opposite of "purity," that "abundance" and "rapidity" are opposites, that "beauty" and "clarity" are opposites. Hermogenes also encourages the use of antithesis in his explanation of the various styles. He says that when the rhetor "can ascribe some rational quality to things that are irrational also produces sweetness,"[28] and that a distinct statement might take the form of antithesis, and that it is part of "subtlety" "not to express cunningly contrived thoughts in a clever way, but to express them simply and directly."[29]

The challenge of correctly utilizing this paradoxical rhetoric becomes clear when Hermogenes warns of a possible mistake: "When the speaker uses rough and vehement or even solemn words to express thoughts that are shallow and commonplace."[30] This is the mistake made by Armado, Holofernes and Nathaniel – the incompetent scholastic rhetors in *Love's Labour's Lost* – who make mundane and stupid observations in the grandest style.

To see how faithful Shakespeare was to Hermogenes, all one needs to do is parse Hamlet's famous soliloquy. In it, Shakespeare uses several of Hermogenes' styles to make his point: clarity, distinctness, solemnity, brilliance and abundance. The first statement "to be or not to be, that is the question,"[31] is antithesis, but also a pure statement, as "purity" "can be used to introduce a topic."[32] It can also be considered as "distinct" because it is setting out what is going to be discussed. Shakespeare then repeats the paradox, this time utilizing an aspect of "grandeur" – "solemnity" – which "involves mentioning the gods or the divine order – [which] removes clear phrases from the commonplace ... and involves how movements of the earth or sea are produced."[33]

It is "solemnity" when Hamlet says "whether 'tis nobler in the mind to suffer / The slings and arrows of outrageous fortune, / or to take arms against a sea of troubles / And, by opposing, end them, to die, to sleep – / No more – and by a sleep we say to end / the heartache, and the thousand natural shocks / That flesh is heir to."[34] "Solemnity" utilizes "long syllables at then end of the sentence … some broad sound that forces us to open our mouth wide when we pronounce it"[35] – which occurs with "outrageous fortune." This passage also involves another aspect of "grandeur" – "brilliance" – because "brilliance is inherent in those acts that are remarkable and in which one can gain luster, or as Herodotus says in which one can 'shine.'"[36] "Take arms against a sea of troubles" is just such a remarkable act.

So the speech goes from a short phrase which is pure and distinct to several sentences that are grand, solemn, and brilliant. The "To Be or Not to Be Speech" then utilizes another aspect of grandeur – "abundance" – which is "breaking something down into its component parts,"[37] nearly halfway through the speech when Shakespeare lists the various ordeals all men must suffer: "For who would bear the whips and scorns of time / Th' oppressors wrong, the proud man's contumely, / The pangs of dispriz'd love, the law's delay / The insolence of office, and the spurns / That patient merit of th'unworthy takes."[38]

That the styles nearly overlap each other is typical of Hermogenes. Hermogenes praises Demosthenes for his masterly mixing of styles. In contrast, Cicero's three categories were related to different genres and occasions. Cicero's three different types of style – high medium and low – were considered to be appropriate for epic, didactic and pastoral plays respectively. In contrast, the seamless incorporation of not just three, but 20 styles *in one speech* is the crux of Hermogenes' approach. Thus the final style "Force" (deinotes) is the ability to use all styles appropriately, and even more importantly, to move from one to another with ease.

Hermogenes was Shakespeare's teacher; this explains a riddle of Shakespeare's style that befuddles critics to this day: his "genre mixing." Most early modern plays were either comic or tragic. One of the barriers to the appreciation of Shakespeare in the 17th century was that in his plays – *paradoxically* – moments of great tragedy occur next to moments of low comedy. Nowadays we find this sudden switch from one genre to another quintessentially modern. But this mixing of genres is clearly a direct consequence of the influence of *On Types of Style*. By urging the rhetor to move often and seamlessly from various high styles (i.e. the category "grandeur") to low ones (i.e. the category of "clarity"), Hermogenes encourages fluidity of genre.

What was Hermogenes' criterion for the application of each style? He states: "Every speech has a thought or thoughts, an approach to the thought, and a style that is appropriate to these."[39] But don't be fooled, though thought is important, "figures of thought" (i.e. metaphors) may be more important still: "Figures of thought, however hold the most important position in the type Force, where they are the most important element of that style."[40] And "rhythm" might be even more important still, than figures of thought: "For one of these factors without the other contributes little or nothing to the style of the speech, but together, in combination with rhythm, they can have a tremendous impact. Musicians, in fact, would probably argue that they are more important than the thought itself."[41]

Hermogenes is suggesting that the rhythm, cadence and word order – the form of the writing – might be more important than the content. But doesn't poetry have something to say? It isn't so much that Hermogenes (and Shakespeare) think that poetry has nothing to say, but rather that the content is the form.

Shakespeare's affection for paradox is ideological. Paradox brings together two opposite ideas that are not resolved, requiring that we think further. We can think beyond paradox of course, but that would lead us to dialectics and the scientific method. Aesthetically, paradox seems to lull us into accepting conflict that has no resolution. This could be seen as alternatively "zen," or just plain nihilistic. Paradox tells us that the world is a confusing place, and that there is not necessarily any order, or answer. Shakespeare's use of paradox says: We live in a world that is full of contradictions, a world which might in fact be godless, or at any rate ruled by pagan Gods that don't have our well-being in mind.

This line of thinking runs very much against the usual notions about Shakespeare. Though Shakespeare scholars now question E.M.W. Tillyard's theory that Shakespeare accepted the orderly universe of the Tudor hierarchy that ran down from God to – let's say – a rock, they are reluctant to consider him as a pagan nihilist. I would suggest that everywhere in Shakespeare's writing is the implication that he refused to idealize man, as God's penultimate creation. Take, for instance:

> What (a) piece of work is man, how infinite in reason, how noble in
> faculties, in form and moving how express and admirable; in action
> how like an angel, in apprehension how like a God: the beauty of the
> world, the paragon of animals – and yet, to me, what is this quintes-
> sence of dust? Man delights not me.[42]

It's not possible to underestimate the significance of the message Shakespeare sends by his persistent employment of paradox. In the above passage Shakespeare foregrounds the paradox that man is a being both infinite in reason and ultimately, a pile of dust. The lack of resolution in all of Shakespeare's paradoxes has impli-cations for the ideals of Christianity and ultimately Aristotle's definition of reason itself, for paradox asserts that one thing can most certainly be another. And Shakespeare asserts this over and over again.

There are other examples that prove that Shakespearean form sends a message stronger than the content. What, for instance, did Shakespeare think about sex? Whole books have been written about Shakespeare's sexual punning. Martin Green's *The Labyrinth of Shakespeare's Sonnets* makes the quite convincing argument that the sonnets are all about sex. In contrast most of the Shakespeare scholarly establishment is suspicious. Stanley Wells asks: "When ... do sexual interpretations proceed from what would once have been considered the dirty minds of the interpreters?"[43] But the fact is that the very form of Shakespeare's work is sexual.

Sloane mentions Demosthenes in the context of "periodic structure." Periodic structure refers to placing subject at the end of the sentence rather than the beginning. Lena Ostermark-Johansen remarks on what Linda Dowling calls the "aesthetics of delay" in Walter Pater: "But perhaps the most striking characterization of Pater's syntax and refined style is Linda Dowling's concept of Pater's aesthetic of delay: 'Pater ... puts off the moment of cognitive closure, not least because it is a little emblematic death. And he does this not simply by writing long sentences, but by so structuring his sentences as to thwart – at times, syntax.'"[44]

This quirk typical of Pater and Shakespeare – this habit of writing sentences in which we don't understand what sentences are about until we reach the end of them – is one of the reasons high school students find Shakespeare's work so frustrating. In *Henry VIII* Anne says: "'tis better to be lowly born / And range with humble livers in content / Than to be perk'd up in a glist'ring grief / And wear a golden sorrow."[45] Anne begins with a subordinate clause, and ends with the subject and predicate. Without such delay tactics the meaning of the sentence is immediately clear: "Having a royal sorrow is more difficult than being low-born and contented."

Dowling's use of the phrase a "little emblematic death" is a reference to orgasm. Sentences which do not reveal their meaning at the outset are sacrificing meaning for sensual delight. One could argue that periodic sentences – by putting off the climax – focus the listener on the meaning. But nevertheless, it's still all about anticipation. Anticipation is pleasing, tantalizing, flirtatious, even sexy – and Shakespeare's writing is chock full of periodic structure. Whether the content is sexual or not (and it often is) the *form* of Shakespeare's work puts sensuality above meaning, in the style of Hermogenes' favourite rhetorician, Demosthenes.

That Shakespeare was conscious of the power of form, that he thought of style as not merely a technique – but an idea – is evident. Take for instance Hermogenes' category of rapidity, or "speed." Shakespeare was familiar enough with rapidity to name a slow-moving character "Speed" in *Two Gentleman of Verona*. "Rapidity" is defined by Hermogenes as "short clauses that develop the thought quickly … saying a lot in a few words."[46]

It is evident that Shakespeare utilized "rapidity" frequently, in witty scenes (Hermogenes associates speed and wit), or simply to just get the plot moving. Trevor McNeely sees "rapidity" as related to Shakespeare's manipulations of time, which sets Shakespeare's apart from other early modern playwrights, since "the theatrical scenes always go by quickly and there are no replays … time in the tragedies and comedies tends to be similarly vague."[47] He continues "time is, or appears to be, treated cavalierly by Shakespeare, "[48] and … "thus dramatic action is conceived as beyond time."[49] McNeely also suggests that Shakespeare's fondness for "rapidity" accounts for "abrupt attitudinal shifts in character, perfunctorily justified at best."[50]

But "rapidity," too, is not just about form, but also about content. In Cecil Wooten's translation of *On Types of Style* Wooten notes that Hermogenes sees "content as the very basis of stylistic effect."[51] Wooten analyzes several passages from Demosthenes' speeches in which the great orator uses rapidity, not just as form, but as idea. For instance: "Rapidity is quite appropriate here since Demosthenes wants to emphasize Philip's energy and activity. In other words, style reflects content."[52] And in contrast Demosthenes uses "abundance" to show "the slowness apathy, and indifference" of the Athenians.[53]

The full implications of Hermogenes' philosophical master-piece become clear in his treatment of "sincerity" (sometimes called "verity," or "truth"). For Hermogenes – even more than Cicero – is obsessed with persuasion, and content is completely dependent on form. Persuasion is not (as in Cicero) merely the goal of high style (the equivalent of Hermogenes' "grandeur"). No, it is the purpose of all rhetoric: all oratory, all art. This conversation between Audrey and Touchstone in *As You Like it* is relevant:

> Audrey. I do not know what 'poetical' is. It is honest in deed and word? Is it a true thing?
> Touchstone. No, truly, for the truest poetry is the most feign-ing, and lovers are given to poetry, and what they swear in poetry may be said as lovers they do feign.
> Audrey. Do wish, then, that the Gods had made me poetical?
> Touchstone. I do, truly, for thou swear'st to me thou art honest. Now if thou were a poet, I might have some hope thou didst feign.[54]

It seems Shakespeare is making a point here, especially since he repeats the words "true" and "feign" (or a variation on them) three times each in a relatively short passage. Touchstone is saying that all poetry is a lie. Similarly, McLuhan paraphrases the patristic philosopher Salutati from the 14th century: "Thus poetry may be outwardly false but essentially true. Holy Writ is of this kind. The origins of poetry are in the foundations of the world."[55]

Does Shakespeare think that poetry is a lie? And if so, does he think, like the grammarian Salutati, that it is "essentially true"? And what does it mean for something to be *essentially* true? Isn't something either true, or it isn't? Shakespeare gives us a hint when he says "the truest poetry is the most feigning." Again, a paradox. But this seems to take Salutati's paradox to an extreme, by suggesting that the poetry which lies the most is also the most *honest* poetry. To propound this riddle, keep in mind that the Earl of Oxford's last name "Vere," means "truth." And the motto of the de Vere family was "nothing is truer than truth." But what in heaven's name does all this talk of "truth" mean, especially when it always seems to be in the context of lies?

It is revealing that Hermogenes' chapter on "verity" is best translated as "sincerity" because that is the way that Hermogenes deals with truth. Truth is whatever you can make the audience believe is true. Truth is whatever you can get away with. Period. Look at what Hermogenes teaches in this chapter. Hermogenes says that "approaches that produce a spontaneous and unaffected style are almost indescribable, but we must try and discuss them."[56] He speaks of the orator losing control as a positive feigning – that if the orator pretends that he has lost control as a speaker, this is very affecting and real, and thus, believable. He also suggests that abusive language can sound very sincere, and that to correct a previous statement, i.e. to pretend to make a mistake and then correct it, makes the speaker appear very honest. He suggests that the speaker is able to gain sympathy by denigrating himself – this is an aspect of humility. This notion of the fallible, humble speaker is so important to Hermogenes that he also takes it up under the category of character. This is not about speaking the truth, but *appearing* to do so. Truth for Hermogenes means the *semblance* of truth.

In *Shakespeare's Sonnets* Shakespeare denigrates himself – or at least the poet – constantly. Sometimes he criticizes his abilities as a poet: "I sometimes hold my tongue, Because I would not dull you with my song."[57] Other times he simply cast aspersions on himself: "I'll myself disgrace, knowing thy will."[58] At times he praises himself too – no doubt about that – but *never* does he praise his powers as a poet for too long without returning to the litany of his own unworthiness as both man and artist. This aspect of the sonnets is one of the most obvious examples of Hermogenes' influence on Shakespeare the rhetor.

Must we then detest Hermogenes and Shakespeare for their addiction to sophistry, to "feigning"? If Shakespeare was a student of Hermogenes, then his goal was to create poetry that was so artificial – if we can interpret Touchstone's notion that the "most feigning" means the most artificial – that it will also be the most true. The only way that this notion is *not* completely despicable, is if we understand that Hermogenes and Shakespeare believed that the very best poetry creates its own truth out of lies. Indeed, the only defence for Shakespeare and Hermogenes, is that – to a master sophist, a great stylist, and a neoplatonic grammarian – poetry is truth.

Shakespeare's favourite paradox – contrasting the outside and the inside, lies and truth, is taken up explicitly by Sonnet 54:

> O how much more doth beauty beauteous seem
> By that sweet ornament which truth doth give!
> The rose looks fair, but fairer we it deem
> For that sweet odor which doth in it live.
> The canker-blooms have full as deep a dye
> As the perfumèd tincture of the roses,
> Hang on such thorns, and play as wantonly,
> When summer's breath their maskèd buds discloses;
> But for their virtue only is their show,
> They live unwooed, and unrespected fade,
> Die to themselves. Sweet roses do not so;
> Of their sweet deaths are sweetest odors made;
> And so of you, beauteous and lovely youth;
> When that shall vade, my verse distills your truth.[59]

The poem is about the external beauty of flowers, which is contrasted with what goes on inside (the "odor"). Roses and wildflowers are both beautiful, but wildflowers are only pretty on the outside, whereas, roses smell beautiful – even when dying: "Of their sweet deaths are sweetest odors made."

Significantly, "truth" is treated as an "ornament" at the end of the second line. Of course we usually think of beauty as an ornament, not truth. Shakespeare challenges us with this new paradox – devaluing truth and exalting beauty, just as in Hermogenes, "truth" (verity, sincerity) is merely a tool that makes beauty more beautiful. Helen Vendler, in her analysis of this sonnet, asserts that "Shakespeare will not admit an unaesthetic truth, truth itself is always aesthetic."[60] In other words, truth is beauty and beauty is truth, and that the truest poetry is the most feigning. Truth is nothing more than the most convincing lie that any artist can come up with – which means the lie that is the most well crafted, and is in that way the most artificial.

The poet (other than Ovid) to whom Shakespeare is most often compared, (and whom he often references in his work) is Virgil. In Leah Whittington's analysis of Virgil and *The Tempest* she speaks of "Virgil's ethically charged aesthetic – in which the authorial voice allows itself to be subsumed into one character's subjectivity and the reader is drawn into an empathetic identification that blurs the distinction between right and wrong."[61]

This applies equally to Shakespeare, whose truth is only the truth of whoever is speaking at the time. And "truth" is only what any poet that can convince us of at any given moment. Annabel Patterson makes an important observation about Hermogenes' attitude to truth and beauty. She acknowledges that he considers them technically, to be opposites, because the style of "beauty" requires ornament, figures of speech, and abundance, whereas "sincerity" is a so-called "naked" style. But for Hermogenes, truth and beauty are "united by persuasion."[62]

Indeed they are. Indeed *we* are. Shakespeare gives us a glimpse of a world where what is most valued is that which is feigned – and to the best liar go the spoils – that is us, the audience, the reader. Beauty is truth. If we find that difficult to understand, or to trust, it's only because we live at a time where language and poetry, fiction and lies, have lost their mystical power.

Was Shakespeare then, an inveterate liar? And was he quite comfortable with the lie that was art? Another paradox; he was, and he wasn't. In plays like *Macbeth* and *The Tempest* Shakespeare says goodbye to poetry and drama. Not without mixed feelings. For Shakespeare – as much as he was a confirmed grammarian, and a student of Hermogenes, and a lover of lies and beauty, and a lover of all lovers and madmen who lie beauteously – was not unaware of Ramus' dire warnings about the dangers of poetic imagery. But it is important for us to understand that Shakespeare proposed an equivalence of truth and beauty. And it is even more important for us to completely understand Shakespeare's love of beauty and lies – before we can understand why – in his later plays – he begged us to say farewell to them both.

Notes

[1] Green, Lawrence D. "Aristotelian Lexis and Renaissance Elecutio" *Rereading Aristotle's Rhetoric* Gloss, Alan and Arthur Walzer (eds.). 154

[2] Patterson, Annabel M. *Hermogenes and the Renaissance*. Princeton University Press, 1970. 216

[3] Green, Lawrence D. "Aristotelian Lexis and Renaissance Elecutio" *Rereading Aristotle's Rhetoric* Gloss," Alan And Arthur Walzer. 153

[4] Ong, Walter J. Ramus, *Method, and the Decay of Dialogue*. Harvard University Press, 1958. 231

[5] Ibid.

[6] Patterson, Annabel M. *Hermogenes and the Renaissance*. Princeton University Press, 1970. 36

[7] Ibid., 37

[8] Ibid., 39

[9] Ibid., 153

[10] McLuhan, Marshall, *The Classical Trivium*. Gingko Press, 2006. 214

[11] Ibid., 236

[12] *Hamlet*. (Folger, 2013) 2.4. 103

[13] Ibid., 2.2. 208-215

[14] Ayers, P.L. "Reading, Writing and Hamlet" *Shakespeare Quarterly* vol 4, #44. 427

[15] Ong, Walter J. Ramus, *Method, and the Decay of Dialogue*. Harvard University Press, 1958. 75-76

[16] *Macbeth*. (Folger, 2013) 1.3.12

[17] Ibid., 1.3.155

[18] Ibid., 1.3.113

[19] Ibid., 1.3.84

[20] *Hamlet*. (Folger, 2013) 3.1. 64

[21] Sloane, Thomas L. (ed). *Encyclopaedia of Rhetoric*. Oxford University Press, 2001. 777

[22] Monfasani, John. *George of Trebizond*. E.J. Brill, 1976. 250

[23] Ong, Walter J. Ramus, *Method, and the Decay of Dialogue*. Harvard University Press, 1958. 211

[24] Conley, Earl Thomas. *Rhetoric in the European Tradition*. University of Chicago Press, 1990. 55

[25] Szakolczai, Arpad. *Comedy and the Public Sphere*. Routledge, 2015. 107

[26] McLuhan, Marshall, *The Classical Trivium*. Gingko Press, 2006. 120

[27] Wooten Cecil W. (trans.) *Hermogenes' 'On Types of Style.'* 43

[28] Ibid., 78

[29] Ibid., 81

[30] Ibid., 108

[31] *Hamlet*. (Folger, 2013) 2.2. 327-332

[32] Wooten, Cecil W. (trans.) *Hermogenes' 'On Types of Style.'* The University of North Carolina Press, 1987. 8

[33]Ibid., 19

[34]*Hamlet.* (Folger, 2013) 3.1. 65-71

[35]Wooten, Cecil W. (trans.) *Hermogenes' 'On Types of Style.'* The University of North Carolina Press, 1987. 26

[36]Ibid., 33

[37]Ibid., 43

[38]*Hamlet.* (Folger, 2013) 3.178-82

[39]Wooten, Cecil W. (trans.) *Hermogenes' 'On Types of Style.'* The University of North Carolina Press, 1987. 218

[40]Ibid., 224

[41]Ibid.

[42]*Hamlet.* (Folger, 2013) 2.2. 327-334

[43]Wells, Stanley. *Looking for Sex in Shakespeare.* Cambridge University Press, 2004. 2

[44]Ostermark-Johansen, Lena. "The Death of Euphues: Euphuism and Decadence in Late Victorian Literature." *English Literature in Transition* 45.1 (2002) 8

[45]*Henry VIII.* Folger, 2004. 2.3 19-22

[46]Wooten, Cecil W. (trans.) *Hermogenes' 'On Types of Style.'* The University of North Carolina Press, 1987. 65

[47]McNeely, Trevor. *Proteus Unmasked.* Lehigh University Press, 2004.139-40

[48]Ibid., 140

[49]Ibid., 141

[50]Ibid., 143

[51]Wooten, Cecil W. (trans.) *Hermogenes' 'On Types of Style.'* The University of North Carolina Press, 1987.

[52]Wooten, Cecil W. (trans.) *Hermogenes' 'On Types of Style.'* The University of North Carolina Press, 1987. 135

[53]Ibid.

[54]*As You Like It.* (Folger, 1997) 3.3 16-26

[55]McLuhan, Marshall, *The Classical Trivium.* Gingko Press, 2006. 158

[56]Wooten, Cecil W. (trans.) *Hermogenes' 'On Types of Style.'* The University of North Carolina Press, 1987. 91

[57]*Shakespeare's Sonnets.* Oxford University Press, 2003. 116

[58]Ibid., 103

[59]Ibid., 68

[60]Vendler, Helen. *The Art of Shakespeare's Sonnets.* Belknap Press,1999. 265

[61]Whittington, Leah. "Shakespeare's Vergil: Empathy and The Tempest." *Shakespeare and Renaissance Ethics.* Cox, John and Patrick Gray (eds). Cambridge University Press. 109

[62]Patterson, Annabel M. *Hermogenes and the Renaissance.* Princeton University Press, 1970. 128

CHAPTER FIVE

Ramus

McLuhan tells us "the complete severance of style and matter in the Ramist rhetoric was a directly contributing influence in bringing about the deliberate impoverishment of poetic imagery after the Restoration. It co-operated with Cartesian innatism to render imaginative or phantasmal experience frivolous at best."[1] Although Shakespeare owed his style to Hermogenes, he could not get Ramus out of his mind. Shakespeare was a devoted rhetorician who wanted desperately to believe the lie of poetry was "truer than truth." But what is piquant about this desire is that Shakespeare, as a student of the neoplatonist Sturm (along with fellow student, Ramus) was painfully aware that beauty's so-called truth could just as well be false.

This is the neoplatonic idea that permeates Shakespeare's work. The neoplatonic paradox is that, although beauty may be a window to ideal forms, it might also be a mistake, and leads us awry. This idea lies at the base of much Shakespearean comedy. Though the platonic perfection of the ideal form might be glimpsed through beauty, it's also possible that beauty might be a lie (hence Titania ends up with an ass). John Vyvyan suggests some artists and lovers "have a more difficult task than others; so that although physical appearance and spiritual reality ought to correspond, and it is inferred they finally will, this is not yet to be expected."[2]

The beauty of the male or female form – as well as the beauty the poet creates in his work – can be deceptive. It could merely be tempting, or it could offer a glimpse of God. How are we to know which? True love is confirmed by meditation and attention to the spiritual mind's eye. But deception is by definition an essential element of a great artist's craft. That is why we fall in love with the wrong people, and why some works of art are dangerous – because they trick us when the appeal is merely superficial.

Shakespeare, when exercising his craft to the utmost, succeeds in delighting and persuading us – even bewitching us – only to undercut it with critiques of language. Shakespeare's early comedies are littered with what I would call "metapoetical" asides, where it seems that the author is lightly yet clearly informing us that his own poetic language is untrustworthy. Viola reminds us in *Twelfth Night*, "they that dally nicely with words may quickly make them wanton."[3] In *Love's Labour's Lost*, the rhetorician Armado is described as "One, whom the music of his own vain tongue / Doth ravish, like enchanting harmony; / A man of compliments, whom right and wrong / Have chose as umpire of their mutiny."[4] And of course there is Touchstone speaking in *As You Like* It of poets who "feign."

These early critiques are due to Shakespeare's neoplatonic leanings which he would have gleaned from Hermogenes and Sturm. In his later plays the comic observations of the earlier plays take a darker turn, and Shakespeare becomes the devil's advocate in what was for him a life-long, and torturous, internal debate. *Must* we reject the imagination? Must we say farewell to beauty? In *Macbeth* and *The Tempest Shakespeare* says – unequivocally – yes. But could Shakespeare be giving ironic expression to the most extreme Ramist opinions of his time? Is he presenting a "counter-argument" to his own Hermogenean poetics, hoping against hope that abandoning the imagination is a project too sad and brutal to be realized?

Why was Shakespeare so obsessed with this paradox of language? Because opposition to poetry and the imagination surrounded him. Anti-theatricalists William Prynne and Stephen Gosson wrote passionately against theatre in the name of Ramism, reading Plato differently than neoplatonists (or from the anti-theatricalists point of view – more accurately). Though neoplatonists equated beauty with truth, in *The Republic* Plato took a very different point of view, castigating art and artists: "The tragic poet is an imitator and therefore, like all other imitators, he is thrice removed from the king and from the truth."[5] And in addition Plato insisted theatrical representations of vice are catching – "lest by imitation they should come to be what they imitate."[6]

So Gosson decrees: "No marveyle though Plato shut them out of his schoole, and banished them quite from his common wealth, as effeminate writers, unprofitable members, and utter enimies of vertue."[7] Joining the loud voices of anti-theatricalists Gosson and Prynne were Sidney and other disciples of Ramus who had transported Ramus' ideas to England; Sidney preaching about poetry's moral purpose in *The Defence of Poesy*, and Harvey propagating Ramist ideas in his pamphlet war with Nashe.

Is it possible that Ramus' ideas could have gotten under Shakespeare's skin and inspired his late, great tragedies? Ramus gutted rhetoric. He removed inventio, dispositio and memoria, (invention, judgement and memory). How might this have specifically threatened Shakespeare's aesthetic?

Ramus' teachings fermented a pedagogical revolution; he changed forever the way philosophy was taught in graduate schools. This movement is eerily familiar; it's much like what is happening in post-secondary education today. A recent article in *The Globe and Mail* says students now flee the humanities for a more practical education in subjects like engineering:

"There is a certain amount of crisis of the humanities talk, that in some cases seems to have preceded rather than followed the decline in enrolments," said Ken Cruikshank, the dean of the faculty of humanities at McMaster University in Hamilton, Ont. "We are up against that perception. Sometimes reversing it is saying OK, you think you need certain kinds of skills. Maybe we can facilitate that."[8]

Walter J. Ong, in his exhaustive study of Ramus (*Ramus, Method, and the Decay of Dialogue*, 1958) offers detailed information and analysis of the early modern philosopher that is difficult to find elsewhere. Ong – though his work predates McLuhan's critique of modern media – is interested in Ramus in much the same way; he sees Ramus' revolutionary movement in relationship to the new technology of the printed book.

Ong says that in the early modern period, the labyrinthine arguments of medieval scholasticism made it imperative to offer students clear and accessible ideas. Thus the criterion for philosophical theory became "not, Is it true? – but is it teach-able?"[9] Pedagogically, Ramism involved a knowledge "something a corporation could traffic in, a-personal and abstract (almost as though it were something which existed outside a mind, as thought one could have knowledge without anybody to do the knowing – as Ramists were eventually to maintain one could)."[10]

Before Ramus gutted it, the three most important categories of rhetoric – invention (knowing what there was to talk about), judgement (knowing what to say about those things), and memory (remembering what one had to say) – involved the observer as much as what was observed. For the rhetorician, all knowledge was filtered through the perceiver and his voice. Ramus, by moving the three main elements of rhetoric to dialectics, made them part of the world outside us, and less human. In fact the world could, and would, continue to exist – whether we might wish to observe it, write poems about it, or not.

Previously inventio was associated with speech and argumentation. But Ramus yanked inventio into the real, perceived world. As Miller summarizes: "Hence Ramus' use of 'invention' in the 'etymological' sense, to mean 'coming upon' or 'laying open to view' not as creating or devising."[11] Miller quotes Ramus: "Ideas are not what they are 'because I discern them; but they are existing, and therefore I discern them.' A concept is not floating in the brain 'a meer fantasme or fantastical thing.'"[12] With this new, dialectical concept of invention, Ramus could plant the seeds for what we know as the scientific method. As Miller explains "it consists of four 'instruments': first, the sense, which perceives; second 'observation' which collects the sense impressions; third 'induction' which notes differences and similarities and abstracts generalizations from singulars; and finally 'experimentia.'"[13]

Ong tells us that – when weighing their importance – old style rhetorician Thomas Wilson rated "judgement or critica or disposition (dispositio) first, and invention second."[14] Ramus not only gave inventio pride of place, he preferred to define dispositio as "arrangement" rather than "judgement." This reflects what Ong sees as the visual aspect of Ramus' dialectics, his preference for arranging arguments according to dichotomies written diagrammatically on the page. These dichotomies were not paradoxes in the Hermogenean sense, but rather arbitrary divisions. Ong gives them little credence, saying they are obligatory nods to the antithetical tradition of philosophy: "The Ramist dichotomies have little, if any real theoretical foundation … it does not arise from any penetrating insight on Ramus' part into the principles of the bipolarity."[15]

According to Ong, the reason Ramus so loved diagrammatic analysis was because of a new technology – the printed book – "Human knowledge for Aristotle exists only in the enunciation, either interior or exteriorized in language."[16] In contrast Ramus failed to "permit any discussion of enunciation at all, [which] is evidence, therefore of the general unconscious veering toward the visual and 'objective' which marks the Gutenberg and post-Gutenberg epoch."[17]

It is the disappearance of dispositio which had the greatest implications for poetry. The seven parts of disposition were exordium, narration, confirmation, peroratio, copia, amplification and decorum. The whole of Hermogenes is devoted essentially to decorum, which focuses on deciding what the appropriate manner of speaking will be. That Ramus and Hermogenes are opposites is confirmed ironically by their attitudes to antithesis. Ramus may have divided his arguments into dichotomies – but this was arbitrary rather than philosophical. When it came down to it, Ramus was suspicious of paradox, that is, he was opposed to *unresolved* contradiction. Though he was often critical of Aristotle, Ramus accepted the Aristotelian proposition of "either/or." Ong paraphrases Ramus – "when two opposites are applied to something by being predicated each of the same subject of the two resulting enunciations, one is true and the other false."[18] A thing can be only one thing, and not another. Period. In Ramus' universe, there was no place for Ovid's magical transformations or Shakespeare's paradoxes.

Ramus also had no time for ambiguity. Ong quotes him on the subject: "Amphiboly and ambiguity of all sorts can generally be disposed of by natural dialectic without the aid of art ... its ability to save a man from double-talking oracles is one of the things which shows clearly the superiority of natural over artificial dialectic."[19]

Probably most important of all, amplification and copia were fundamentals of rhetorical practice and intrinsically connected with ambiguity. Trousdale reminds us that the great humanist rhetorician Erasmus defined copiousness as "desirable expansion of a topic … [because] nature rejoices in variety."[20] Copia involves the use of examples, questions, details, and lists to elaborate on any topic, and is the technique favoured by Shakespeare (in "to be or not to be" and many other places as well). Trousdale goes on – "not a tightly structured pattern of events … but a rich copia of thoughts and words overflowing in a golden stream."[21]

Trousdale also reminds us that a fundamental aspect of copia involves not only a plethora of words, but also of meanings. She remarks on "the artist's ability to allow all possible significances to be drawn from his tale and through his verbal artistry to invite us to do the same."[22] Without copia, Shakespeare would have had nothing to write, and his work might have been more available to the ravages of unrelenting Ramist exegesis.

Indeed Shakespeare's poetry could not have existed in a world of impoverished Ramist rhetoric. The Ramist "plain style" is the very opposite of Shakespeare's. The "plain style" was the lean and clear prose associated with puritan sermons. It was expected to convey God's moral truths without ambiguity. For puritan enthusiasts of the plain style, all oration and poetry could be whittled down to its premises, to what was informative in a logical or scientific way. One of the reasons some people find Shakespeare so frustrating – and so many students wish he would just "come out and say it" – is because we live in an anti-rhetorical, scientific world, that has no patience for the more mysterious, ambiguous perceptions that we might find in Shakespeare.

Like Ramus, we are suspicious of what is permanently obfuscative and manipulative. We all like a good mystery; but we want it to be solved. As Ong tells us, for Ramus, poetry is a dead thing "the art is itself a dead surface, a web of lifeless precepts … it is the business of use to draw out into a work these precepts in a way which will shape and express in examples the force contained within the precepts."[23] Ramus does what many a bad English teacher does, removing from a poem the frippery, the decoration, the ornamentation, the copia, the metaphor, the paradox, to get to the meaning. Ong describes Ramus' definition of a poem: "An oration or poem stripped down to its essentials is a string of definitions and divisions somehow or other operating through syllogisms."[24]

Shakespeare's writing is resistant to such insanely logical exegesis. Perhaps deliberately so? One can find plenty of ideas lurking beneath the surface of any Shakespeare play – but woe be it to the person who attempts to draw from Shakespeare's poetry a particular point of view – or even attitude – to almost anything. Shakespeare presents us with a multitude of paradoxes and opposing arguments, period. It's tempting to think that Shakespeare wrote in this style deliberately to spite Ramus. We must assume that a well educated writer like Shakespeare would be aware of Ramus' tampering with inventio or disputio. But even if we somehow posit that Shakespeare had little formal education (which seems doubtful in the light of his learned style), his Hermogenean roots are true to the pre-Ramist, grammarian tradition.

It is evident from Shakespeare's later plays that Shakespeare was not only aware of Ramus' tampering with memoria, but significantly traumatized by it. Why would memoria be important to Shakespeare? Memoria is the ancient "art of memory" that Francis Yates so eloquently explains in her book of the same name. When Ramus moved memoria into dialectics, he transformed memory – *from an art* – into memorizing words and diagrams on a page.

And for the early moderns, memory was not simply memory. *Memory WAS the imagination.*

The rhetorical process involved remembering things, of course. One could invent ideas or arguments (inventio) and then choose how to categorize them and utilize them (disputio). But when it came time to speak a eulogy – for instance – it was necessary to remember all that one had to say. The "bible" for memory was the *Ad Herennium* – originally attributed to Cicero, but now acknowledged to be of unknown authorship. It is the oldest western rhetorical source, probably from the late 80s B.C. The *Ad Herennium* outlined a method of memorization which may surprise you.

I was compelled to memorize a number of facts for my Ph.D. comprehensive exam, and I had a system. But because I am *not* an early modern rhetorician, the method I chose was related to the printed page. That is why I can't remember those facts today. Those ideas fade from memory just as the printed pages and their diagrammatic systems – the boxes, asterisks and arrows – fade too. But Frances Yates makes clear that imagining a printed page was not the preferred method of memorization in an oral culture. Here she describes the favoured early modern technique:

> The artificial memory is established from places and images ... A locus is a place easily grasped by the memory, such as a house, an intercolumnar space, a corner, an arch, or the like. Images are forms, marks or simulacra [formae, notae, simulacra] of what we wish to remember. For instance if we wish to recall the genus of a horse, of a lion, of an eagle, we must place their images on definite loci.[25]

If one wished to remember a large number of things, one had to have a large number of places in one's head. The student was responsible for inventing his own images for remembering things; this was a private process. This notion of memory explains where the modern expression "in the first place" comes from. The student of rhetoric would have many old houses, buildings, public institutions, etc. – with many rooms for storing images – inside his "mind's eye." The "mind's eye" is a phrase most likely made popular by Shakespeare. The term came into common usage after

Hamlet used it to answer Horatio. Hamlet is asked how he can have seen his dead father. He answers: "In my mind's eye, Horatio."[26] It's important to remember that, whenever Shakespeare speaks of "ghosts," he means us to reference the "mind's eye" and our imagination.

When the rhetorician needed to remember new speeches, the images that had been in the rooms were erased and replaced by a new set of images. Yates observes: "What strikes me most about them is the astonishing visual precision with they imply. In a classically trained memory the spaces between the loci can be measured, the lighting of the loci is allowed for."[27] But even more striking yet were the images themselves. For the rhetorician was not simply to place "any old" image in his mind's eye. Yates reminds us that Cicero wrote that the image would have to be singular, and extreme – which means both extremely horrible or extremely beautiful:

> [I]f we see or hear something exceptionally base, dishonorable, unusual, great, unbelievable or ridiculous that we are likely to remember for a long time … We ought there to set up images of a kind that can adhere longest in the memory … if we assign to them exceptional beauty or singular ugliness; if we ornament some of them, as with crowns or purple cloak so that the similitude may be more distinct to us, or if we somehow disfigure them, as by introducing one stained with blood or soiled with mud or smeared with red paint, so that its form is more striking.[28]

Disfiguring images? Staining them with blood? What *are* these images? They seem very much like something from a modern horror movie. Or pornography perhaps? Sarma quotes Yates, in turn quoting Ravenna – a 15th century jurist – on his memory practice: "I usually fill my memory-places with images of beautiful women which excite me more … if you wish to remember quickly, dispose the images of the most beautiful virgins into memory-places."[29]

Ramus, as Yates tells us, specifically targeted these memory practices:

> Ramus abolished memory as a part of rhetoric, and with it he abolished artificial memory ... one of the chief aims of the Ramist movement for the reform and simplification of education was to provide a new and better way of memorizing all subjects. This was to be done by new methods whereby every subject was to be arranged in dialectical order. This order was set out in schematic form in which the "general" or inclusive aspects of the subject came first.[30]

What is most striking, though, is not simply Ramus' substitution of one method for another, but his disapproval of imagination. Ramus was a Protestant convert, a Huguenot, killed in the St. Bartholomew's Day Massacre. This martyrdom increased his popularity with puritans after his death. For Ramus – propagator of the "plain style," desecrator of ornament and metaphor, hater of the "mind's eye," enemy of the poet's imagination – poetry was a graven image to be righteously destroyed in the name of God. Sarma paraphrases Yates:

> According to Yates this prohibition of graven images taken from the fourth chapter of Deuteronomy was interpreted by Ramus as applying to the classical art of memory as well. The rhetorical traditions quite actively advocated the use of lewd and grotesque images by which to excite the imagination and empower the memory, which to Ramus, was tantamount to a systematic technique for polluting one's mind.[31]

That Hermogenes and Sturm were very much opposed to Ramus on this issue is clear from their association with Camillo. Yates tells us that neoplatonist Camillo invented a colossal monument to memoria in his Memory Theatre:

> One of the most striking manifestations of the Renaissance use of the art is the Memory Theatre of Giulio Camillo. Using images disposed on places in a neoclassical theatre – that is using the tech-

nique of the artificial memory in a perfectly correct way – Camillo's memory system is based (so he believes) on archetypes of reality on which depend secondary images covering the whole realm of nature and of man.[32]

A three dimensional model of Camillo's Memory Theatre may or may not have existed. His deathbed description of the theatre was published after his death in 1550 in *L'idea del Teatro*. At first Camillo was to build his memory loci into an image of a human body, but later he decided to illustrate them as the seats of a theatre, with the possibility of rotating each row of seats so that different combinations of images could occur. The images were related to various religions, Kabbalistic, Hebrew and Christian – as well as astrology. The mystical number 7 is featured strongly in his idea of Camillo's memory theatre, and the rhetorician could have in his mind's eye, as *The Art of Memory* suggests – "the eternal order of the universe."[33] Yates speculates that Camillo's theatre "involved also an interest in the rhetoric of Hermogenes … Johannes Sturm, so important in the new movements, carried on the revival of Hermogenes. And Sturm certainly knew of Giulio Camillo."[34]

Camillo, Sturm, Hermogenes and Shakespeare were neoplatonists; Ramus was not. The dividing line for Ramus was Plato. Ramistic anti-theatricalists utilized Plato's *Republic* to attack poets, and Ramus was clearly anti-neoplatonic, at least according to Ong: "The Platonic idea that the sensible world is ephemeral and the world of spiritual or exemplar realities eternal does not appear as a passionate belief in Ramus' thought … Nor does Platonism make itself felt as an exaltation of intuitive knowledge over knowledge arrived at by more pedestrian processes."[35]

Ramus' philosophical innovations were an attack on the imagination. But how can we be certain that Shakespeare was upset by his teachings? Well, for one thing, Shakespeare and

Ramus used the same terminology to refer to imagination. Ramus said that an idea was not a "meer fantasme or fantastical thing." The word "fantasme" – usually spelled "phantasme" – was common in rhetorical circles and usually meant dream, or invention of the mind. *The word "phantasms"* as well as the word "phantastical" are utilized by Shakespeare and associated with *The Arte of English Poesie* (attributed to George Puttenham, 1589), a book on courtly rhetoric fashioned after Castiglione's *The Book of The Courtier.*

The 16th century courtier faced a turning point in his identity. Previously courtiers were primarily warriors, but in the 1500s the European courtier was encouraged to be a poet/rhetorician as well. In Elizabeth's court, where poetry, drama and wit were praised, Castiglione's book was highly prized. William Rushton's analysis in *Shakespeare and The Arte of English Poesie* enumerates the many instances when Shakespeare appears to take Puttenham's advice, utilizing the very words – and sometimes, in his plays, naming the figures of speech – mentioned by Puttenham. McNeely quotes Puttenham, noting that the salient feature of the *Art of English Poesie* is that it unabashedly associates poetry with deception:

> [T]herefore leaving these manner of dissimulations to all base minded men, ... we do allow our Courtly poet to be a dissembler only in the subtilties of his art: that is, when he is most artificial, so to disguise and cloake it as it may not appeare, nor seeme to proceede from him by any studie or trade of rules, but to be his naturall.[36]

For Puttenham, the poet was an artful liar in the sophistic tradition, and the more artificial his lies the better. So the activity that was condemned by Ramus was openly embraced by the courtier poet Shakespeare; the artful pursuit of lies. William Rushton tells us Puttenham uses the word "phantasies" in the *Art of English*

Poesie, associating it approvingly with the poetic imagination, saying such things are "all manner of beautiful vision by which the inventions of the mind are much helped, as without it no man could devise any new or rare thing."[37] It is no surprise that Holofernes in *Love's Labour's Lost* – if he is a caricature of the Ramistic Harvey – rails against the very same thing: "I abhor such fanatical phantasimes, such insociable and point-devise companions."[38]

The word "phantastical" appears in *Macbeth*. After Macbeth hears the witches' first prediction, and is beginning to ponder the possibility of murdering the king, he comments on the frightening turn of his own train of thought: "My thought, whose murder yet is but fantastical, / Shakes so my single state of man / That function is smother'd in surmise, And nothing is but what is not."[39]

This is the essence of Macbeth's dilemma: "Nothing is, but what is not." Throughout the play we come to understand that Macbeth is not so much being overtaken with a lust for power as becoming entangled in the fantastic thrall of an imagining which ultimately blots out reality. Shakespeare goes to enormous lengths to convince us that Macbeth is losing his mind, stressing that he is clearly the furthest thing from a cold-blooded killer. Macbeth's hesitation is not so much a moral issue as an epistemological one. The debates that he has with himself have little to do with morality, and much to do with his fear that ambition has caused him to lose his hold on reality. If Shakespeare had wanted us to learn a moral lesson from Macbeth, he would given Macbeth this final speech provided by bardolator David Garrick:

> Tis done! the scene of life will quickly close. Ambition's vain delusive dreams are fled. And now I wake to darkness, guilt and horror; I cannot bear it! let me shake it off – it will not be; my soul is clog'd with

blood – I cannot rise! I dare not ask for mercy – It is too late, hell
drags me down; I sink, I sink, – my soul is lost forever! Oh! – Oh![40]

Instead of such musings on morality, Macbeth ponders a much
more frightening dilemma: he can no longer trust his senses. He
sees a knife that is not there: "Is this a dagger which I see before
me, / The handle toward my hand? Come let me clutch / thee. I
have thee not, and yet I see thee still."[41] Shakespeare goes on, in
the fashion of copia, to say the same thing in various ways: "Art
thou not, fatal vision, sensible / To feeling as sight ? Or art thou
but / A dagger of the mind a false creation / proceeding from the
heat obsessed brain?"[42]

Lady Macbeth is under a similar spell, and when she reads
Macbeth's letters she no longer lives in the present, but in the future
of her imagination: "Thy letters have transported me beyond / this
ignorant present, and I feel now / The future in the instant."[43] This
seems more like madness, a disease (and indeed Lady Macbeth
does go mad). They are both mad with imagination.

We are asked to ponder not so much the moral choices made
by Macbeth and Lady Macbeth as to contemplate their madness.
One can only blame the witches for that (Lady Macbeth never
meets the witches, but she seems like somewhat of a witch herself, possessing their gender fluidity).

And what sort of beings are the witches? What is most
important about the witches is not that they have beards like
men, or make toad brews that lure sailors to their deaths. It is
their speech that ultimately hypnotizes Macbeth. Their speech is
as profound and confusing as double speaking oracles associated
with Apollo and condemned by Ramus. The visions the witches
create and the poems they recite are fantasies of the imagination
that Macbeth fatally misinterprets.

Critics have consistently bemoaned the presence of the
witches as a device not worthy of Shakespeare. Samuel John-

son attempted to quell his own dis-ease with Shakespeare's use of "enchantment" by suggesting that Shakespeare incorporated magic spells "his audience thought awful and affecting."[44] Yes, the witches *would* be unworthy of Shakespeare – and inappropriate for the tragedy of *Macbeth* – *only if* Shakespeare had been a little more concerned with Macbeth's moral dilemma rather than the fantasies swirling around in his brain.

The witches show Macbeth three visions in the fire: an armoured detached head, an aborted baby, and child wearing a crown. These images are certainly as bloody and bizarre as those rhetoricians were encouraged to use for their memoria loci. Macbeth tells us that the witches equivocate; which means they lie to tell the truth. Equivocation was a technique associated with the traitorous Catholic Jesuits (considered pariahs in Early Modern England) used to escape persecution; lying outwardly but telling the truth to god. As master equivocators the witches are "feigning" poets.

Macbeth calls the witches "imperfect speakers"[45] and Banquo asks "can the devil speak true?"[46] observing: "The instruments of darkness tell us truths / Win us with honest trifles, to betray's / In deepest consequence."[47] Banquo describes the utterances of the witches much the way Thomas Nashe describes poetry. According to McLuhan, Nashe's notion of poetry was that it must be misleading and dark. As mentioned earlier, Nashe speaks of "blinde fables and dark stories," and "in poems the things that are most profitable, are shrouded under fables that are most obscure."

Shakespeare achieves a monumental feat of rhetorical manipulation in his last plays by utilizing "indignation" – a technique that Hermogenes categorizes under "sincerity." In "sincerity" or "truth" – in actuality the art of *appearing* truthful – the rhetor denigrates his own powers:

> Indignant thoughts are created even out of those that seem modest, whenever they are approached in such a way that the speaker willingly gives up some of his own advantages or agrees to yield to the advantage to his opponent or, from what he says in his speech obviously deems himself or his opponent worthy of deeds or words that are opposite of those stated. Ironic statements are like this, and they clearly involved the use of a certain approach: "Perhaps someone wants to think me mad. For it is probably madness to attempt something beyond one's means." In this passage he has created Indignation by calling his ambition madness.[48]

What's striking about this passage is that in his definition of indignation Hermogenes seems to be directly referencing Macbeth, a character whose dire deeds (and thoughts) are almost bearable because he frames himself as in the grip of madness.

Hamlet, Macbeth and Lear, and arguably, Othello, are all mad. All of them are deluded by their imaginations. When Shakespeare wears the mask of Macbeth, he is asking us to eavesdrop and sympathize on the thoughts of someone who commits horrific, amoral crimes. As masks for Shakespeare all of these anti-heroes are self-denigrating. In other words, Shakespeare's heroes, instead of being perfect men, are highly imperfect ones who create perfect worlds with language. So Shakespeare only makes his argument for poetry through these humble, flawed persona. Shakespeare, in his late plays, is wearing the mask of a self-denigrating madman, utilizing Hermogenes' "indignation."

Wearing the mask of Macbeth, Shakespeare eloquently expresses his dissatisfaction with himself and all poets as dissembling witches. And he longs for the ancient, perfect "grammarian" Eden in which poetry was the pure word of God. When Macbeth asks the witches what they are doing at the cauldron they reply: "A deed without a name."[49] Here, the witches are perverting the magical origins of epistemology, the mystical law of names. One of the reasons why grammarians thought it was possible to read the world through poetry was because – and here

McLuhan quotes Cratylus – "I believe Socrates, the true account of the matter to be, that a power more than human gave things their first names, and that the names which were thus given are necessarily their true names,"[50] and similarly, from Genesis – "And whatsoever Adam called every living creature, that was the name thereof."[51] At the dawn of time, before Adam's fall, everything had a true name, because words were true, and words reflected the truth of the world; now poetry is deceptive and untrustworthy, as is language.

Shakespeare is furiously mourning the grammarian idealization of an ancient, holy perfect language; this is the tragedy of Macbeth. This is why Macbeth's most moving lines at the end of the play are not about his wrongdoing, his guilt, or his redemption. At the end of his life Macbeth decries the emptiness of his own life in terms of the vacuity of the present state of poetry, which can only be a reflexive, self-lacerating reference by Shakespeare to himself, the poet, in the "indignant" style – as he is the poet who has supplied the words that Macbeth and the witches speak.

Does Shakespeare actually sympathize with the Ramist notion that language is corrupt? No. But in the ultimate gesture of Hermogenean "sincerity," a mad murderer curses language with virulent eloquence, longing for a time when language made sense. This is the epitome of sophistical manipulation. Once, everything had a true name, and words were the perfect mirror of truth. Once signs in poetry had mystical meaning; now poetic signs cannot be understood, life is merely: "a tale / Told by an idiot, full of sound and fury, / Signifying nothing."[52] For Shakespeare this failure of language is the stuff of tragedy. For if poetry must end, then so must he.

Here Shakespeare masters the art of Hermogenes' sincere style. How can we doubt Shakespeare's sad idealization of poetry

– through the perverse mask of Macbeth? He has masterfully denigrated himself in the Hermogenean manner. He is defamed himself, more even than he does in *Shakespeare's Sonnets*. Shakespeare – *because he is a poet* – is Macbeth, is the witches, is Lady Macbeth, like all of them, he is caught in an evil web of dissembling poetry.

In a Ramistic universe, in a culture in which the very nature of sophistic lies were under attack – when Puttenham was encouraging courtly poets to lie artfully at the same time as Ramistic anti-theatricalists demanded closure of the "amoral" theatres – Shakespeare's sophistic stance was the one he picked to be the most manipulative, the most persuasive. The only way that Shakespeare could deeply honour poetry – in a period where poetry was so suspect – was to decimate it, wearing the mask of an imperfect madman and killer who simultaneously manages to offer us a chilling eulogy for a perfect poetry that was long gone. And we listen, because Macbeth is so flawed, and painted so perfectly with the persuasive brush of Hermogenes' indignation.

In *The Tempest*, Shakespeare takes the notion that "if poetry dies, then so must I!" – to its logical conclusion.

Let's just say that Shakespeare wanted his final play to be an ode to poetry that could persuade even the most staunch opponent of art. With those intentions, he could have written a play about a virtuous, loving, honest poet and playwright who is under attack from anti-theatricalists, and Ramist poets like Sidney, but who commits suicide because he so very much loves poetry. The plot would be a series of scenes in which his friends and family try and persuade the poet not to commit suicide – leaving us in suspense about the outcome. But alas, at the end of the play, the poet takes his own life; not without a series of heart wrenching odes to the beauty of poetry.

This play would have represented Shakespeare's real sympathies. The play could have been persuasive in the manner of Cicero's rhetoric – that is we would hear both sides of the argument. The anti-Shakespeare, anti-florid poetry characters representing Gosson and Sidney would have their say in this play – and speak of the perils of poetic styles that are too ornamental and seductive. But our sympathies, of course, would be with the gracious, kind, dying sophist.

That is the play that Shakespeare would have written if he had read only Cicero and not Hermogenes. Instead, Shakespeare's first task – in the style of Hermogenes' "indignation" – was to create a leading character that was not essentially sympathetic, a character who could have given Shakespeare, the author, the humility that Hermogenes requires for a perfect orator.

After years of bardolatry, and of interpreting *The Tempest* as autobiographical – and therefore a flattering – representation of a sweet and sympathetic old businessman/grain merchant (i.e. Shakespeare himself), critics have convinced most of us that Prospero is a kindly father figure in a sweet fairy tale. Frank Kermode sees the slave Caliban as a representation of natural magic and the fallen nobleman Prospero as a representation of spiritual magic. However, in terms of the conflict between the two, he says Caliban's "parents represent an evil natural magic which is the antithesis of Prospero's benevolent Art."[53] In this interpretation, Prospero is associated with his fairy sidekick Ariel, who represents the airy neoplatonic ideal, and Caliban the grimy, murky mud of the body – sex and death. There is only one problem with this interpretation. It ignores what is actually going on in the play.

Lytton Strachey noted of *The Tempest* that "if Prospero is wise, he is also self-opinionated and sour, that his gravity is often another name for pedantic severity, and that there is no character in the play to whom, during some part of it, he is not studiously disagreeable."[54] Prospero's magic involves manipulating people in the most ethically questionable ways, raising the spectre of their own death and then suddenly removing the threat. When we first meet him, he is being confronted by his daughter about the storm that he has caused. He reassures her that no one is killed in the storm – "there is no soul – / no not so much perdition as an hair / Betid to any creature on the vessel."[55]

The problem with Prospero's defence is that his victims don't know "what is real and what is not" (in the manner of Macbeth). He is also not only punishing a man who has wronged him – on the ship is the King of Naples who stole his crown – but many innocent people who happen to be on the ship also: *women and children who have done nothing wrong*. Not only does Prospero torture people, but he quite enjoys it, in the manner of a 19th century moustache-twirling villain.

When he creates a magical dinner for Alonso and the conspirators Antonio and Sebastian, Ariel appears as a harpy, and scolds them. Prospero is very proud: "My high charms work, and these mine enemies are knit up in their distractions. They are now in my pow'r."[56] Ironically, we have no proof that Antonio and Sebastian learn anything from their "amazement" – for though the King of Naples has a neat conversion and redemption at the end of the play (almost too neat to be believed, in fact), Antonio, Sebastian, Trinculo, Caliban and Stephano all seem curiously unrepentant and will probably continue to get up to no good if they can manage it. Prospero's magic primarily serves his own needs, it doesn't offer much redemption or moral uplift (in the Ramistic manner) for mankind, or the audience.

On top of all this Prospero is not, in his personal life, a terribly kind man. He puts his own daughter and her innocent, virtuous young suitor Ferdinand through various torturous emotional machinations to make sure that (in the neoplatonic manner of the comedies) they are seeing beyond physical beauty into the beauty of their souls. Are we to imagine that locking up Ferdinand in a cage (to apparently teach her daughter's lover "a lesson") is *not* sadistic, is *not* mean-spirited? And when it comes to "the spirit" – it is far from clear that Prospero represents pure soul in opposition to Caliban's deformed body.

Prospero treats Caliban with brutal physical savagery; he curses him and then beats him like an animal. But this part man / part fish Caliban offers some of Shakespeare's most beautiful poetic allusions to poetry itself: "Sometimes a thousand twanging instruments will hum about mine ears, and sometimes voices / that if I then waked after long sleep will make me sleep again; and then in dreaming / methinks the clouds methought would open and show riches / Ready to drop upon me, that, when I waked, / I cried to dream again."[57] On the other hand, it is true that Miranda claims Caliban tried to rape her. But, paradoxically, at the end of the play, Prospero takes responsibility for Caliban's evil nature and calls it his own: "this thing of darkness I / Acknowledge mine."[58]

So Shakespeare manages, in Hermogenean fashion, to create a leading character who is not a "good man" but an extremely flawed one; and a perfectly humble rhetorical avatar. But how can he speak for poetry when he is a magician and not a poet?

There is no doubt that Prospero is essentially a poet and dramatist. In the second scene of the play (between Prospero and Miranda) Shakespeare uses the word "art" 4 times – spoken once by Miranda and three times by Prospero himself. In addition, each time Prospero uses the word "art" it has a different meaning. What could be a more obvious clue to his dissembling, poetic nature? Marjorie Garber raises the question: "Does Prospero stand for all mankind or just one side of the argument – if the first it is a colonialist play, if the second it is a play about art and creation."[59]

Prospero is a caster of spells and maker of dreams. He mentions that he was trained in the "liberal arts"[60] and Orgel notices (in his introduction to the play) that an important aspect of Prospero's magic is "theatre, illusionism, the unserious delight implied by Prospero's characterization of his masque as 'Some vanity of mine art.'"[61]

Even Frank Kermode sees Prospero as, essentially, a theatrical director: "Prospero plays the part of a masque presenter ... The characters are thoroughly manipulated by the presenter ... The plot of *The Tempest* leads up, without hesitation or uncertainty, to that moment when Prospero gathers his forgiven enemies around him, [and] draws back the curtain before the inner stage."[62] The only reason that Shakespeare makes Prospero a magician and not a poet, is because magicians clearly manipulate people, fool them, trick them, pull the wool over their eyes. Magicians are essentially dissemblers.

But there is also another reason.

Shakespeare's technique in creating Prospero is not as straightforward as creating a theatrical avatar (as he did in *Macbeth*) who is wildly imperfect and ultimately speaks poetically, in favour of poetry. What is radically Hermogenean about *The Tempest* is that Shakespeare puts Hermogenes' notion of marrying form and content into ingenious practice. Of course Prospero speaks beautifully and movingly, but it is through the form of the play that he manipulates us. Prospero is awfully entertaining, not only because of what he says, but because of what he does. We never know quite what he is doing to do next, and his antics are sometimes as exciting for us as they are painful for the victims of his fictions.

But because Prospero is a magician who manipulates people, we get not only to see the artist at work, but to enjoy his creations.

The situations the characters get up to are due to Prospero's manipulations (in other words, Shakespeare's manipulations). Prospero even speaks like an artful dramaturge. When he decides to throw obstacles in the way of the courtship of Ferdinand and Miranda, he speaks as a playwright might speak about adding plot complications for the leading characters: "They are both in each other's powers. But this / Swift business / I must make uneasy, lest too light winning / Make the prize light."[63]

The play becomes metatheatrical; the medium is the message. We *the audience* are manipulated by Prospero. So when Prospero threatens to stop using his magical powers, we know that these delightful characters, the airy melancholy Ariel, the naive and earnest Miranda, the tortured and virtuous Ferdinand, the moaning doglike Caliban and all the rest – will also vanish forever – or at least until we go and see another production of *The Tempest*. In this Hermogenean manner Shakespeare has his cake and eats it too. For no one could accuse him of writing an ode to poetry. No, poetry is dead. Prospero killed it. There you are, Petrus Ramus. Okay, my poetry didn't teach Antonio and Sebastian a lesson. It was simply enchantment, frippery, lies beauty? "So it's gone now," says Prospero. "I've killed it. Are you happy?"

Shakespeare gives us something much more potent than an ode to poetry. Instead of an ode to poetry, he offers up a eulogy: "But this rough magic / I here abjure, and when I have required / Some heavenly music, which even now I do, / To work mine end upon their senses that / This airy charm is for, I'll break my staff / Bury it certain fathoms of the earth, / And deeper than did ever plummet sound / I'll drown my book."[64]

But no, the audience does not wish to say goodbye to the fictive world that Shakespeare has created. By managing to involve the audience in the comedy and drama of the play, and then threatening to take it all away, Shakespeare convinces the audience – some of them against their will, certainly – that they must mourn for the death of poetry. And then, at the end he beseeches them to applaud him: "Now I want spirits to enforce, art to enchant, / and my ending is despair / Unless I be relieved by prayer / Which pierces so that it assaults / Mercy itself, and frees all faults. / As you from crimes would pardoned be, / Let your indulgence set me free."[65]

What does Prospero have to be forgiven for, if he is a good man? Well, he is a liar, poet and dissembler. There are doubts as to whether or not Shakespeare actually wrote this epilogue, but in my view there can no doubt that he did. And it does not matter if he did not, because it is such an eloquent continuation of the sophistical argument of the play. For puritans or Ramists in the audience the appeal to God at the end would stick in their craws. For here was a play filled with phantasms of the most lewd and evil variety. And yet the entire audience would have found themselves clapping to keep Prospero alive in their imaginations. Because Prospero was after all, like all of us, nothing more than of "such stuff / As dreams are made on."[66] Shakespeare created an argument that was so eloquent and manipulative, that *no one* could disagree with him. And he managed to write a eulogy for poetry; ensuring us that we would miss it, even if it was not yet gone. And in spite of ourselves – and that is the point of it all, really – we weep.

Notes

[1] McLuhan, Marshall, *The Classical Trivium*. Gingko Press, 2006. 192-3

[2] Vyvyan, John. *Shakespeare and Platonic Beauty*. Chatto and Windus, 1961. 44

[3] *Twelfth Night*. (Folger, 2009) 3.1 14-15

[4] *Love's Labour's Lost*. (Folger, 2009) 1.1 170-173

[5] Jowett, Benjamin (trans.) *The Republic – Plato*. The Floating Press, 2009). 666

[6] Ibid., 193

[7] Gosson, Stephen. *The School of Abuse*. The Shakespeare Society, 1841. 10-11

[8] Chiose, Simona. "As Students Move Away from the Humanities Universities Adapt" *The Globe and Mail* 3 March, 2017 https://www.theglobeandmail.com/news/national/as-students-move-away-from-humanities-programs-universities-adapt/article34207300/ accessed Feb 27 2019

[9] Ong, Walter J. . *Ramus, Method, and the Decay of Dialogue*. Harvard University Press, 1958. 23

[10] Ibid., 152

[11] Miller, Perry. *The New England Mind in the 17th Century*. Harvard University Press, 1939. 148

[12] Ibid.

[13] Ibid., 149

[14] Ong, Walter J. . *Ramus, Method, and the Decay of Dialogue*. Harvard University Press, 1958. 112

[15] Ibid., 199

[16] Ibid., 108

[17] Ibid.

[18] Ibid., 210

[19] Ibid., 191

[20] Trousdale, Marion. *Shakespeare the Rhetoricians*. University of North Carolina, 1982. 46-47

[21] Ibid., 69

[22] Ibid., 141

[23] Ong, Walter J. . Ramus, *Method, and the Decay of Dialogue*. Harvard University Press, 1958. 190

[24] Ibid., 192

[25] Yates, Francis A.. *The Art of Memory*. Random House, 2011. 22

[26] *Hamlet*. (Folger, 2013) 1.2. 193

[27] Yates, Francis A.. *The Art of Memory*. Random House, 2011. 24

[28] Ibid., 25

[29] Sarma, Gopal P. "The Art of Memory and the Growth of the Scientific Method" 16 www.researchgatenet.publication/243963957 accessed 30 June 2018

[30] Yates, Francis A. *The Art of Memory. Random House*, 2011. 229

[31] Sarma, Gopal P. "The Art of Memory and the Growth of the Scientific Method" 16 www.researchgatenet.publication/243963957 accessed 30 June 2018

[32]Yates, Francis A. *The Art of Memory*. Random House, 2011. 51

[33]Ibid.

[34]Ibid., 230-231

[35]Ong, Walter J. . *Ramus, Method, and the Decay of Dialogue*. Harvard University Press, 1958. 206

[36]McNeely, Trevor. *Proteus Unmasked*. Lehigh University Press, 2004. 73

[37]Rushton, William Lowes. *Shakespeare and the Arte of English Poesie*. Forgotten Books, 2015. 52

[38]*Love's Labour's Lost*. (Folger, 2009) 5.1. 18-20

[39]*Macbeth*. (Folger, 2013) 1.3 152-155

[40]Williams, William Proctor. "In Production: Macbeth through the Years." *Macbeth: Shakespeare in Performance*. 3-4

[41]*Macbeth*. (Folger, 2013) 1.5. 42-47

[42]Ibid., 1.5. 48-51

[43]Ibid., 1.6. 64-66

[44]Johnson, Samuel. "Macbeth" *Macbeth* (Signet Classic: 1998). 124

[45]*Macbeth*. (Folger, 2013) 1.3. 73

[46]Ibid., 1.3 113

[47]Ibid., 1.3 136-138

[48]Wooten, Cecil W. (trans.) *Hermogenes' 'On Types of Style.'* The University of North Carolina Press, 1987. 98

[49]*Macbeth*. (Folger, 2013) 4.1. 50

[50]McLuhan, Marshall, *The Classical Trivium*. Gingko Press, 2006. 15

[51]*The Bible*. (Genesis, 2:19)

[52]*Macbeth*. (Folger, 2013) 5.5 29-31

[53]Kermode, Frank (ed.). "Introduction" *The Tempest*. Methuen, 1962. xv

[54]Strachey, Lytton. *Books and Characters*. Harcourt, Brace, 1922. 68

[55]*The Tempest*. (Folger, 2015) 1.2. 36-38

[56]Ibid., 107-110

[57]Ibid., 3.2. 150-156

[58]Ibid., 5.1. 330-331

[59]Garber, Marjorie. *Shakespeare After All*. Doubleday, 2008. 852

[60]*The Tempest*. (Folger, 2015) 1.2. 73

[61]Orgel, Stephen (ed.). *The Tempest*. Oxford University Press, 1987. 21

[62]Kermode, Frank (ed.). "Introduction" *The Tempest*. Methuen, 1962. lxxiii

[63]*The Tempest*. (Folger, 2015) 3.1. 542-545

[64]Ibid., 5.1 58-66

[65]Ibid., 5.1(E) 13-20

[66]Ibid., 4.1. 173-174

CHAPTER SIX

Sexuality

"About all that one can get out of the sonnets, considered as transcripts of experience, is the reflection that pederastic infatuations with beautiful and stupid boys are probably very bad for practicing dramatists."[1] One can only assume that when he wrote this, Northrop Frye was having a bad day. It seems cranky and ill-considered, and it's not true. Frye is forcing a Ramistic analysis on Shakespeare. Yes, of course, if we are compelled to boil the sonnets down to a moral imperative then it would have to be a principle that is both scandalous and banal at the same time, i.e.: "Falling in love with stupid, beautiful boys is a bad thing." But Shakespeare would not be interested in such a reductive analysis. And who says that Shakespeare was trying to accurately transmit his "experience"? As master rhetorician, his goal may have been to contrive the most convincing fantasy possible.

For what relationship did the content of Shakespeare's work have to his life? What, after all, is the relationship of any writing to life, of form to matter? It might be more relevant to consider the musings of the great post-Aristotelian rhetorician Scaliger who proposed that the characters in Virgil's *Aeneid* really existed: "Poetry *seems* as if another God, to construct real things."[2] Perhaps Shakespeare's characters are not transcripts of his experience, or portraits of specific people. Perhaps they are inventions of the imagination that are so lively and appealing that – for some – *they actually exist*. When the play is over, we mourn them like the passing of a dear friend.

Much that is of very little value has been said – on the subject of Shakespeare's sexuality, because the vast majority of the sonnets (126 of 154) are addressed to a young man, who is beautiful *on the outside*. Whether or not he is also beautiful *on the inside* is a matter of much poetic conjecture in the sonnets themselves. Because of this, many critics feel they must explain the content of the sonnets, or explain it away.

Shakespeare establishment critics such as Stanley Wells and Northrop Frye dismiss the notion that the sonnets have anything to do with Shakespeare's sexuality. They are right to do so; we have no idea what the sexuality of the man from Stratford might have been – no matter who the sonnets are dedicated to. And when it comes to a candidate for Shakespeare named Edward de Vere – the fact that one of his enemies accused him of fiddling with a castrato is hardly proof of anything. Foucault tells us that before the trials of Oscar Wilde there was no such thing as a homosexual person; there were only homosexual acts: "The sodomite had been a temporary aberration; the homosexual was now a species."[3]

And yet one of Shakespeare's contemporaries was a poet who explicitly took as his subject matter same sex love. Richard Barnfield is best known for two books: *The Affectionate Shepherd* and *Cynthia with Certain Sonnets*. A quote from The Affectionate Shepherd is somewhat shocking even today: "Scarce had the morning starre hid from the light / Heavens crimson canopie with stars bespangled, / But I began to rue th' unhappy sight / Of that faire boy that had my hart intangled; / Cursing the Time, the Place, the sense, the sin; / I came, I saw, I viewd, I slipped in."[4] This is not coy; it is explicit.

Barnfield apologized for his homoerotic poems in his second collection – using the excuse that he was imitating Virgil's pastoral *Second Eclogue*. But his second collection, too, contained homoerotic poetry. Barnfield's poems are more explicit and less complex than Shakespeare's. So if Barnfield "came right out and said it" – why didn't Shakespeare? The answer probably has less to do with the moral climate of early modern England than it does with Shakespeare's chosen rhetorical style.

Make no mistake, homosexuality was illegal in early modern England. Henry VIII instituted the death penalty for sodomy, which, as Goldberg tells us, had an expansive early modern definition – "any sexual act, that is, that does not promote the aim of married procreative sex (anal intercourse, fellatio, masturbation, bestiality)."[5] And yet Orgel suggests:

> Homosexuality in this culture appears to have been less threatening than heterosexuality, and only in part because it had fewer consequences and was easier to desexualize. The reason always given for the prohibition of women from the stage was that their chastity would thereby be compromised, which is understood to mean that they would become whores. Behind the outrage of public modesty is a real fear of women's sexuality, and more specifically, of its power to evoke men's sexuality.[6]

Orgel is right to say that fear of women's sexuality was rampant. Stephen Greenblatt goes so far as to suggest that for Elizabethans there was only one gender – the male gender – as medical textbooks viewed women's sexual organs as internalized male ones. Greenblatt also speaks of fear of women: "We can secure the self only through a restraint that involves the destruction of something intensely beautiful; to succumb to that beauty is to lose the shape of manhood and be transformed into a beast."[7] The fear was that female sexuality might overpower the male and consequently destroy him. Today some straight men fear homosexuality, but celebrate the "playboy." But in early modern culture the ultimate threat to masculinity was not homosexuality but the fear that men's desire for women (and women's desire for men) would make men womanish. This is the reason that boys played women's roles on Shakespeare' stage.

And the demonization of sodomy was not as negligible as Orgel seems to suggest. Though Foucault theorizes that the modern homosexual didn't appear until the trials of Oscar Wilde, sodomy was associated with effeminacy. Ramist anti-theatricalists, for instance, linked them together. Prynne suggests in Histriomastix: "Men's putting on of woman's raiment is a temptation, an inducement not only to adultery, but to the beastly sin of Sodomy, which ... is most properly called adultery, because it is unnaturall."[8]

Harvey, puritans, and Ramists were deeply homophobic. Harvey dismissed de Vere satirizing his "Italianate" nature. This description of de Vere (from Nelson) suggests sodomy – as Italy, unlike England, was thought to be the land of sodomites: "No wordes but valorous, no workes but woomanish onely. For life Magnificoes, not a beck but glorious in shew, In deede most friuolous not a looke but Tuscanish always."[9]

This association of *Shakespeare's Sonnets* with sodomy prevailed after Shakespeare's death. When Benson published the sonnets in 1640 (the preferred edition for 140 years), he reversed the genders of three of the poems, and Schiffer tells us that Stevenson (a Shakespeare editor from the 1600s) said the phrase "master mistress of my passion" caused "disgust and indignation."[10]

Today one method of explaining the content of the sonnets is to suggest that the poet's idealization of a beautiful boy is related to neoplatonism. Imagining love in the shape of a boy isolates the spirit, because the love of a man for a young man's body would be impossible (i.e. unimaginable). Certainly neoplatonism permeates Shakespeare's work, but that doesn't explain why he chose the "boy love" metaphor. Other humanist sonneteers such as Wyatt and Petrarch did not. The tradition of the young man as representation of pure neoplatonic spirit was found in Virgil's pastorals, which – when Barnfield emulated them – were viewed as sodomitical.

It's also important to note that Shakespeare's poems – if not clearly explicit – are nevertheless suggestive. Sonnet 20 has caused much discussion, especially the ending: "And for a woman wert thou first created, / Till nature as she wrought thee fell a-doting, / And by addition me of thee defeated, / By adding one thing to my purpose nothing."[11] On the surface this seems to mean that the young man, because he has a penis ("nature … fell a-doting") is of no sexual use to Shakespeare. But why even entertain the possibility that a young man *might* be another man's sex object, in a purely heterosexual universe? And the word "nothing" was Elizabethan slang for vagina. (When Hamlet asks Ophelia what she is thinking, she says "nothing," and he says: "That's a fair thought to lie between maids' legs."[12])

Shakespeare's Sonnets are not the only place to find same sex desire in Shakespeare. The love of Antonio for Sebastian in *Twelfth Night* is similar to the idealization of the young man in the sonnets. Critics like to explain away Antonio's expression of his "love" for this gentle young man as merely friendship. This is a young man who looks exactly like his sister, and admits that he cries like his mother at the drop of a hat. Paul Hammond asks us (in Figuring *Sex Between Men from Shakespeare to Rochester*) why, if this is simply friendship, are the stakes so high; why does Antonio say: "If you will not murder me for my love, let me be your servant"[13]; and why does Sebastian reply: "If you will not undo what you have done – that is, kill him whom you have recovered – desire it not."[14]

If they love each other as friends, why is their talk of their love a life and death issue? There is also another Antonio – in *Merchant of Venice* – who loves a young man named Bassanio.

Salonio says of Antonio's feelings for Bassanio: "I think he only loves the world for him."[15] Bassanio says that he loves Antonio more than his wife: "Antonio, I am married to a wife / Which is as dear to me as life itself; / But life itself, my wife, and all the world / Are not with me esteemed above thy life, / I would lose all, nay sacrifice them all / Here to this devil, to deliver you."[16]

There are other instances in Shakespeare's plays in which male characters love one another deeply. But ruminations of this sort are necessarily perilous, because we are utilizing a Ramistic approach. Shakespeare most likely meant many, all, or just some of the associations and resonances that are precipitated by his poetry. And one never knows the motives of the deniers. W.H. Auden – a closeted homosexual – famously damned those who interpreted the sonnets as "gay": "The homosexual reader, on the other hand, determined to secure our Top-Bard as the patron saint of the Hominterm ... preferred to ignore those [sonnets] to the Dark Lady."[17] However, discussions about the meaning of *Shakespeare's Sonnets* are as "bottomless" as the discussion of Shakespeare's sexuality.

More significantly, Shakespeare's style is distinctly reminiscent of his contemporary John Lyly. And Lyly's writing was associated with effeminacy. And since the bardolators have insisted that Shakespeare is the quintessential poet in English, the possibility that he might be associated with effeminacy leaves the door open to tainting *all* the arts and humanities with the effeminate brush. This has made it necessary to disassociate Shakespeare from euphuism – a style that clearly influenced Shakespeare.

The euphuistic style of writing was all the rage in England in the 1570s. Euphuism is usually associated with John Lyly, the grandson of eminent grammarian William Lyly – who wrote the grammar textbook that was commonly used in Tudor schools. William Lyly was friends with great humanist Thomas More.

John Lyly thus had familial ties to the most eminent grammarians of the 16th century. He also had a connection with Edward de Vere. Both were closely associated with Lord Burghley – De Vere was of course Burghley's ward, and Lyly is said to have "attached" himself to Burghley.

Eventually, Lyly – who was unable to have much success at university, and was much reviled by scholastics such as Harvey – became Edward de Vere's secretary. After publishing two enormously popular novels – *Euphues or The Anatomy of Wit* and *Euphues and His England* – Lyly turned to writing plays for St. Paul's School. The plays were also very popular and performed with casts of all boy actors – students at St. Paul's. This was the school for which John Lyly's grandfather William Lyly had been first master.

Traditionally scholars have gone out of their way to disassociate Shakespeare and Lyly, in fact, by stressing that Shakespeare's work is more substantial than his clearly "effeminate" counterpart. True, Lyly is no Shakespeare. But it's almost as if Lyly writes like a young Shakespeare; his work seems like a testing ground for the rhetorical techniques Shakespeare perfected. It would certainly be inaccurate to say that the two writers are *not at all* stylistically connected. In fact they echo each other.

Scholars have long suggested that Shakespeare makes specific reference to Lyly's style in his works as *parody* – suggesting Shakespeare had a bemused tolerance for a lesser artist. Andy Kesson's recent book on Lyly suggests that in fact the modern image of Shakespeare has been based on the disparagement of Lyly: "The denigration of Lyly's work in the eighteenth and nineteenth centuries has been an important part of the formation of the Elizabethan canon,"[18] and "in the eighteenth century Lyly is repeatedly described as an infection or disease for which Shakespeare was the cure."[19] Even bardolator David Garrick felt it necessary to praise Shakespeare at the expense of Lyly.

In his 1632 introduction to Lyly's plays, E. Blount states: "All our Ladies were then his Schollers; And that beauty in Court, which could not parley Euphueisme was as little regarded, as she which now there speaks not French."[20] Croll says: "Euphuism is a style characterized by figures known in ancient and medieval rhetoric as schemes (*schemata*) or more specifically word schemes (*schemata verborum*), in contrast to tropes, that is to say, in effect by the figures of sound."[21]

Word schemes are here separated from more poetic figures of speech – such as metaphor – by their appeal to the ear. Examples are *isocolon* (use of phrases of the same length) *parison* (use of corresponding words of the same type, such as nouns or verbs), *paromoieon* (similarity in the sound of words, either similar at the beginning (*alliteration*) or at the end (*homoiteleuton*), as well as the *repetition* of words, or elements of words. Lyly's novels are written in prose, and resemble the style used by patristic fathers for Latin sermons, except that the are written in English. In other words, euphuism is about the subtle aural patterning of prose that makes prose sound poetic. It was popular because it gave the "vernacular" English language all the prestige of traditional Latin eloquence.

This is the definition of euphuism that has come down to us from Morris W. Croll and G.K. Hunter. Both suggest that Lyly's excessive concern with purely vocal ornamentation differentiates his work from Shakespeare's. According to them, Lyly's ornamentation was used *only* for sense effect, whereas *all* of Shakespeare's devices always shape the meaning of the text. This is not entirely true; Shakespeare sometimes creates pleasing sounds for their own sake, and Lyly's appealing sounds are certainly *not merely ornamentation*. And Shakespeare utilizes many of Lyly's euphuistic schemes.

It's easy enough to find similarities between the styles of Shakespeare and Lyly. A passage from *Romeo and Juliet* is often quoted as an example of Shakespeare parodying Lyly. Euphuism is characterized by listing countless examples. This is the favourite humanist rhetorical technique of copia; saying the same thing over and over again, in different ways. From Lyly's *Euphues* we have this modest list: "The shoemaker must not go above his latchet, nor the hedger meddle with anything but his bill."[22] Shakespeare takes much the same comparison and muddles it to comic effect imitating the excess of some of Lyly's lists: "It is written, that the shoemaker should meddle with his yard, and the tailor with his last, the fisher with his pencil, and the painter with his nets."[23]

This might very well be a parody of Lyly. But Rushton's *Shakespeare's Euphuism* (1871) provides more than 100 instances of concurrences between both words and subject matter in Shakespeare and Lyly. One striking example mentioned by Rushton is the use of chameleon as metaphor – evidence that Lyly used not only figures of sound but figures of speech. Geron's metaphor in Lyly's play *Endymion*: "Love is a chameleon, that draweth nothing into the mouth but air, and nourisheth nothing in the body but lungs"[24] seems nearly identical to Hamlet's notion here: "Excellent 'i' faith, of the chameleon's dish: / I eat the air, promise crammed: you cannot feed capons so."[25]

Such correspondences are to be found everywhere. For instance Orsino's famous exhortation from *Twelfth Night*: "If music be the food of love play on, / Give me excess of it, that, surfeiting / The appetite may sicken and so die / That strain again! It had a dying fall"[26] is significantly similar to Endymion's entreaty: "Father, your sad music being tuned on the same key that my hard fortune is hath so melted my mind that I wish to hang at your mouth's end till my life end."[27]

And compare Hamlet's soliloquy – "To die, to sleep – / No more – and by a sleep to say we end / The heartache and the thousand natural shocks / That flesh is heir to – 'tis a consummation / Devoutly to be wished. To die, to sleep – To sleep, perchance to dream"[28] to Endymion's soliloquy – "No more, Endymion, sleep or die. Nay die, for to sleep it is impossible and yet I know not how it cometh to pass, I feel such heaviness in mine eyes and heart that I am suddenly benumbed. It may be weariness, for when did I rest? It may be deep melancholy, for when did I not sigh?"[29]

A much deeper correspondence can be found in the subject matter. The subplot of Lyly's *Endymion* concerns Sir Tophas, a comic knight who – like Sir Toby in *Twelfth Night* – *is not* a very brave or admirable character. Sir Tophas' paradoxical situation is that he must decide between war and poetry. His dilemma is a comic version of Hamlet's tragedy of inaction, and also echoes Harvey's exhortation to de Vere to give up the pen for the sword. Sir Tophas falls in love with an old woman (Dipsas) and is quite unmanned by his feelings: "Love hath, as it were, milked my thoughts and drained from my heart the very substance of my accustomed courage. It worketh in my heat like new wine, so as I must hoop my sconce with iron, lest my head break and so I betray my brains … Take my gun, and give me a gown."[30] Tophas' problem echoes the early modern obsession with emasculated men.

The disturbing spectacle of women humiliating paragons of masculinity – specifically male warriors – is a common trope in Shakespeare. Three Shakespeare tragedies revolve around this situation: Antony is unmanned by Cleopatra, Macbeth is unmanned by Lady Macbeth, and Coriolanus is unmanned by his mother. It could be argued that *all the rest* of Shakespeare's tragic heroes are unmanned – Hamlet is unmanned by his mother, Lear by his daughters, and Othello by his wife. G.K. Hunter quotes Petrarch's complaint that the new humanist courtier was less a warrior than effeminate poet: "Where do we read that Cicero or Scipio jousted?"[31]

Most of Shakespeare's romantic males are revealed as ridiculous, though often sympathetic, objects of satire. Of course Shakespeare is an equal opportunity satirist – sometimes female characters (like Titania and Helena) love as ridiculously as men. But it is the entire project of *Love's Labour's Lost* and *Merry Wives of Windsor* to enjoy the spectacle of women ridiculing men and ultimately ruling them. Men are unmanned because they cannot stop desiring.

In the climactic fourth act of *Love's Labour's Lost* the courtiers recite their own lovesick sonnets as the others watch and make fun of them. Berowne will have none of it; he compares them all to fallen warriors, likening the experience to seeing "great Hercules whipping a gig, / And profound Solomon to tune a jig, / And Nestor play at pushpin with the boys."[32] At the moment when Berowne is most swelled with pride at his ability to avoid what seems like an infectious disease of effeminate lovesickness, Costard arrives with a love letter that is signed by Berowne himself. Berowne too, is unmanned: "That you three fools lacked me fool to make up / the mess / He, he and you – and you my liege – and I /Are pickpurses in love, and we deserve to die."[33]

The women agree to meet the men in disguise – and consequently ridicule them for being confused about which women they are in love with. Boyet characterizes the women as warriors armed with words "conceits have wings / Fleeter than arrows, bullets, wind, thought, swifter things."[34] The women, in fact, are the more skilled warriors. What follows is a pageant of "nine worthies." One weak-kneed scholar after another steps forward to ineptly portray a great warrior of history. Holofernes concedes that Moth, being so small, represents "Hercules in the minority."[35] By the end of the *Love's Labour's Lost* the men surrender to the women. Berowne says: "Our wooing doth not end like an old play. / Jack hath not Jill."[36]

It is, as usual, difficult to pinpoint Shakespeare's attitude to all this. One can imagine a happy early modern (or for that matter 21st century) audience of manly men enjoying the play. Sexist men may see *Love's Labour's Lost* as a comic warning not to let women gain the upper hand. But it's odd that Shakespeare would painstakingly chronicle the tragi/comic destruction of the male gender in so many plays – if he wasn't somewhat on the side of male effeminacy. One could certainly understand the puritan reaction against theatre in the context of – not only the goings-on in the dressing rooms, but – the subjects of the plays themselves. Many of Shakespeare's plays focus on the spectacle of men who refuse to act like men. Keep in mind that any Shakespearean mention of cuckolding seems to guarantee laughter, and such jokes are ubiquitous in the plays. If plays teach as well as delight – or if, as Plato suggests, we may become infected by what we imitate – what then?

Jocelyn Powell quotes several critics of euphuism who associate euphuism with a disease. The vogue of euphuism was sometimes compared to an epidemic: French Professors Legouis and Cazamian in their history of English literature labelled it "a disease of language."[37] (Before that it had been labeled an "infection" by post-Restoration playwright Colly Cibber, among others.)

What is the significance of this association between a literary style and an infectious disease? In her essay *The Death of Euphues: Euphuism and Decadence in Late Victorian Literature*, Lena Ostermark-Johansen focuses on the demonization of euphuism in the later part of the 19th century. She contends that euphuism was forgotten for years and promptly weaponized in the late nineteenth century against decadent poets such as Oscar Wilde. She says "charges of foreignness, effeminacy, and of a false focus on manner rather than matter were frequently raised against such writers as Swinburne, Rossetti and Pater, and the term "Euphuism" was invoked to illustrate the ridiculous extremes to which such concern with verbal ornament could be taken."[38] Ostermark-Johansen quotes Pater's assertion that *Love's Labour's Lost* and Shakespeare's Sonnets were euphuistic:

> It is so with that old euphuism of the Elizabethan age that pride of dainty language and curious expression, which it is very easy to ridicule, which often made itself ridiculous, but which had below it a real sense of fitness and nicety; and which, as we see in this very play, and still more clearly in the Sonnets, had some fascination for the young Shakespeare himself. It is this foppery of delicate language, this fashionable plaything of his time, with which Shakespeare is occupied in 'Love's Labours [sic] Lost.'[39]

Pater loved euphuism; and he was Wilde's philosopher of choice. Ostermark-Johansen quotes a late 19th century contributor to MacMillan's Magazine who complained about literary effeminacy: "Manliness is not just at this moment the capital distinction of our literature either in prose or verse … In the general bulk of our original work this quality of manliness is certainly not conspicuous."[40] This lack of "manliness" was also associated with euphuism by those who wished to defend Pater: "Mr. Pater was not a 'simple' writer. Indeed – dreadful thought! – was he not a 'euphuist'? Was he not mannered and very sugary? Was he, indeed, quite 'manly'? I cannot resist asking by what literary council has it been decided, as an absolute law, that writing must be always simple, unmannered, unadorned, or, indeed, so-called 'manly'?"[41]

There could be many reasons for this insecurity about the gender associations of euphuism. Elizabethan ladies were very attached to euphuism, and the court of Elizabeth was pervasively feminine. G.K. Hunter observers: "The court of Elizabeth was neither natural nor free, its ritual was artificial to the last degree. The sovereign was a painted idol rather than a person. The codes of manners it encouraged were exotic, Petrarchan and Italianate."[42] Indeed, plays like Endymion (about a man who falls in love with woman who is the moon) and poems like *Venus and Adonis* (about an older woman who effectively rapes a young man), have been associated with Elizabethan anxiety over being ruled by a female. *Euphues: The Anatomy of Wit* concerns a young man who travels to Italy and is so bewildered and tortured by women that he runs home to England for refuge.

But it was not only the subject matter of Lyly's work that caused anxiety. Lyly attempts to redeem his content: Although much of his first novel focuses on a young man being manipulated by women in Italy, when he returns to England he "finds religion" and becomes a much more conservative, less lovesick, and in this sense a much less "Italianate" (and consequently less depraved) person. If Lyly wished to "cover his ass" in terms of the moral content of his novel, this was a valiant attempt. No; no matter what the subject matter, it was Lyly's style that was the disease; and the disease associated with it was effeminacy.

It is no surprise the vogue for Lyly came and went so quickly. Harvey and other Ramus disciples attacked and dismissed him. Lyly was the "anti-Ramus." Child speaks of "the enmity Lyly and he [Harvey] had for one another,"[43] which found its manifestation in the duelling pamphlets of the Martin Marprelate controversy. Lyly represented for some, the epitome of humanist rhetoric, of concern for form over matter. Hunter quotes Erasmus, who expresses quite blatantly the notion that style is more important than ideas: "They are not to be commended who in their anxiety to increase their store of truths, neglect the necessary art of expressing them."[44]

Lyly – with his concern for ornamentation – was the enemy of all Ramism. And in the early modern period some saw ornamentation as both feminine and depraved, as well. Croll quotes early modern critics of patristic sermons: "Blessed be god that we now see one sermon ... which can be read without a tune or an effeminate prattle of consonance."[45] Croll also mentions the rhetorician Wilson who criticized the abuse of schemes in minstrels "which in lieu of weightiness and gravitie of words has nothing to offer but wantonness of invention."[46]

What became a problem in both sermons and euphuism was the Ramist contention that ornamented poetry was more concerned with language than with reality. There is much "nature" in Lyly, but it is the "nature" that is to be found in poetry – specifically in Latin bestiaries devoted to the poetic significance of various bizarre and often imagined representations from the animal kingdom. These animals often have no relationship to observations of the real world. The "chameleon" metaphor utilized by both Lyly and Shakespeare is a perfect example. Chameleons do not live on air. This mere fact did not bother Lyly or Shakespeare, for the image was nonetheless gripping, sad, and a bit scary, and therefore persuasive; and one that was probably to be found in both Shakespeare and Lyly's memory "loci."

This is what separates medieval and early modern poetry from modern poetry. Over the years, the trajectory of modern education in the humanities, the university study of English as subject, and the art of poetry itself have become more and more "scientific." Shakespeare's style is significantly unscientific and significantly unrelated to any reliable observation of the world around us. This is not only reflected in Shakespeare's choice of metaphors but in the salient stylistic features that effectively characterize both writers: the use of antithesis, and the unreliability of the narrator.

Lena Ostermark-Johansen speaks of alliteration and antithesis as Lyly's most favoured stylistic techniques for endowing English prose with the beauty, grace and eloquence of poetry which was borrowed from Petrarchism: "Euphues' long soliloquies on love … are a glorious display of the rhetoric of the divided mind."[47] Both Lyly and Shakespeare are obsessed with presenting opposing sides of unresolved arguments. Ostermark-Johansen also quotes Devon Hodges, who seems to agree with me that Shakespeare's use of paradox challenges traditional approaches to understanding the text, and making sense out of it. He suggests that antithesis – as paradox, as utilized by Lyly (and I would argue, Shakespeare) – works to destroy the meaning of the text, its *utility*, that is, the text's ability to be read as a moral tract, or even merely as narrative information:

> Though antithesis provides an authoritative and obvious method of organization, it also frustrates the linear development of the narrative and its ethical goals. A characteristic passage from the love soliloquies shows both how antithesis controls Lyly's language and how it fragments meaning. In a world where reciprocity is prohibited by antithesis, soliloquy is the ideal form of communication. In a soliloquy, the self doubles and opposes itself.[48]

In addition to this, one must note the use of the Hermogenean technique of sincerity – on the part of both Lyly and Shakespeare – which requires that the speaker denigrate himself. Lyly was certainly one of the first unreliable narrators. Lyly opens his second novel with a self-denigrating reference to the first one: "In faith Euphues, thou has told me a long tale The beginning I have forgotten, the middle I understand not, and the end hangers not together."[49] Kesson says: "Lyly opens his story by warning his readers to suspect and interrogate stories."[50]

Lyly's narrator is as unworthy and unreliable as the narrator of *Shakespeare's Sonnets*. In fact there is something playful about Lyly's tone which reminds one of *Shakespeare's Sonnets*. All this self consciousness points to the author's invention and seems to suggest that poetry is merely play, merely one person's flawed musings, take them or leave them. And we have seen Shakespeare, in his plays, wearing the mask of many different flawed characters, making it quite impossible for us to know with whom to identify or what to believe.

Trevor McNeely goes one step further and suggests that Shakespeare's errors are intentional, and they point to the artificiality of his work. There are many such errors that have been duly noted, particularly anachronisms. For instance, Hamlet has just returned from school but then is also described by the gravedigger as being thirty years old. Joan of Arc (in *1 Henry VI*) can appear twenty years after she is dead to be present at the death of Talbot. Also there were no clocks or billiards in ancient Rome – but these objects appear in *Julius Caesar* and *Antony and Cleopatra*. McNeely suggests that these are not mistakes, but that instead Shakespeare wishes to draw our attention to his artistry, his manipulations, to make his rhetorical technique evident: "Shakespeare is showing us how we are being manipulated."[51] This "showing off" is also, paradoxically, a confession of vulnerability on the part of the author, lest you think his manipulations are real. Shakespeare is in effect saying: "I know you may have been so carried away by my stories that you have mistaken them for reality. In case you see me as God, I am not. I am a flawed human being, as my obvious errors will make clear."

This confession is, paradoxically, both humble and boastful. The stories are just stories – and fabricated, and fantasy lacks the perfection of reality, as McNeely reminds us here, quoting Murrin: "The story must remain incomplete or absurd, if the poet wants to let truth shine through his picture veil."[52] This self consciousness about the writer's skill goes beyond Lyly's admission of fallibility or the self-denigration by the author of *Shakespeare's Sonnets*.

I would not go so far as to suggest that Shakespeare and Lyly are writing "tongue in cheek" (although Susan Sontag has accused Lyly's work of being "camp"). But the very fantasticalness of Shakespeare's and Lyly's conceits and – if McNeely is right, Shakespeare's intentional mistakes – are metatheatrical reminders of the ancient practice of the art of memory. McNeely quotes Edgar Wind: "For we remember the absurd more easily than the normal and the monster often precedes the God."[53] Things that are strange and improbable are clearly imaginary, not real.

This tendency to move as far from the real perceived world – and to self consciously acknowledge that distance – has been gendered by western culture. After Oscar Wilde was sent to prison for the crime of gross indecency, some serious literature in the west took a turn away from fantasy, euphuism and effeminacy. Wilde was perhaps imprisoned not only for his sexual indiscretions, but for the implications his sexuality had for aesthetics.

Scottish jurist and Liberal MP Haldane visited Wilde in prison. He recommended that Wilde's ordeal might morally improve him, and consequently inspire him to write something of depth and importance: "suggesting he had not used his literary gift to its full force because he had dissipated himself in a life of pleasure. Now misfortune might prove a blessing for his career, for he had got a great subject."[54]

By 1920 there was a new philosophy of writing that originated in the theories of writers like Pound, William Carlos Williams, and Hemingway, which – unlike Wilde's euphuistic style – was overtly and concentratedly concerned with reality, as opposed to fantasy. Pound, Hemingway and Williams found great subjects for their work. That great subject was reality itself. This was a direct response to a more feminine style, which was deliberately obfuscative, and whose use of antithesis frustrated the possibility of exegesis (and perhaps reason) and whose tone challenged the credibility of its own observations. One major school of 20th century writers believed that their writing should be – if not always lean – then certainly unadorned, with a direct connection to reality itself. And this point of view was pointedly male.

Wyndham Lewis's new aesthetic philosophy – named "Vorticism" (1913-15) by Ezra Pound – was, according to Elizabeth Oliver, a reaction to Wildean decadence. Poetry was held to have "carried negative connotations of effeminacy, passivity, weakness and homosexuality. These associations developed in the years after Oscar Wilde's trial for gross indecency."[55] And "Ezra Pound shared Lewis's hatred of decorative aesthetics, returning almost obsessively to the problem of verbal ornament in his prescriptive writings on poetry."[56] Vorticism exhorted writers to "employ always the exact word, not the nearly exact, not the merely decorative word."[57] Oliver mentions that, for the 20th century masculinist school of writing, it was not even fashionable for *female* writers to be feminine.

That decoration was associated with women becomes clear from Vorticist reviews of Marianne Moore, a poet who was approved of by the Vorticists, due to her apparent "literary masculinity": "Moore, working with the modernist sphere of production, had a special interest in distancing the technical achievements of poetry from 'decorative women's work.'"[58] Oliver quotes Lisa Tickner who speaks of "modernism's penchant for ... male display ... For these men, art was not a domestic pastime, but a primate battle fought to the death."[59] Vorticism was related to Imagism (founded by Pound and William Carlos Williams) which was obsessed with clarity and precision of language in poetry.

This is a far cry from Oscar Wilde's articles in women's magazines, obsession with poetic ornamentation, defence of "lying," and proud remark that he had to "live up" to his blue china. One can see this in the work of 20th century feminist theorists like Simone de Beauvoir and Hélène Cixous. Cixous dismisses the "classic representations of women (as sensitive – intuitive – dreamy, etc.)."[60] For De Beauvoir, the difficulties women writers face have their origins in femininity: "They believe their worth comes from an inner grace, and they do not imagine that value can be acquired; to seduce, they know only how to display themselves: their charm works or does not work."[61] For De Beauvoir the problem with women's writing was due to their lack of opportunity to exist in the real world, which precipitates their inability to *write about* the real world: "They will not abandon themselves to the contemplation of the world: they will be incapable of creating it anew."[62]

Ernest Hemingway's work is the epitome of the 20th century masculine writing style. Hemingway is so masculine that the revelation that he may have had doubts about his own masculinity, becomes, in itself, a hallmark of maleness. In his essay on Hemingway's style, Harry Levin relates various anecdotes re: the universal perception that Hemingway was effortlessly masculine: "Herein it is reported by John Groth that 'Hemingway's jeep driver knew him as Hemingway the guy, rather than Hemingway the famous writer.' And Mr. McCaffery devotes his particular enthusiasm to 'Hemingway as a man among men.'"[63]

And this evaluation of Hemingway's masculinity was inevitably associated with his sparse, lean style. In the same article, Alfred Kazin associates Hemingway's precision with a relationship that must exist between the word and the world: "He gave a whole new dimension to English prose by making it almost as exact as poetry, by making every word sound, by reaching for those places of the imagination where the word and the object are one."[64] Hemingway becomes in this sense, the modern "scientific" writer, as Levin continues: "Critics – and I have in mind Wyndham Lewis – have called his writing 'the prose of reality,'"[65] and ... "he has been attempting to restore some decent degree of correspondence between words and things; and the task of verification is a heavy one, which throws the individual back on his personal resources of awareness."[66]

This is a very influential writing philosophy that has dominated aesthetics since the early part of the 20th century. This writing asks us to focus a world that we all seem to know, one that is definitely "there." "We all know what that world is," is what Hemingway seems to say – and he might go on to say – "and don't give me any of that dreamy feminine crap that says we don't!" The only problem, says Hemingway and his ultra-masculine buddies, is that we don't look at the world closely enough, or see it clearly enough, or report on it accurately enough. Remember: Hemingway started his career as a reporter.

This attitude to the art of language is exactly the opposite of the medieval grammarian poet's conception of the art – for one simple reason. Creating reality is quite different from observing it. The difference is a fundamental, epistemological one. The "effeminate grammarian" assumes that each of us creates our own reality, whereas the "lean masculine modern writer" assumes that there is a reality "out there" and all we need to do is observe it. This is also the difference between post-structuralism and the enlightenment. Post-structuralists – along with medieval grammarians – would have us regard enlightenment modes of perception with suspicion. They, like Shakespeare, would have us nurture a healthy scepticism about the notion of "reality." After all, we are all prejudiced observers with different points of view. Like Shakespeare, the self-denigrating author of the sonnets, and the characters who are Shakespeare's anti-hero/avatars in so many plays – we are all flawed and perhaps deluded.

The history of the world changed fundamentally with the enlightenment and the scientific method. Before the enlightenment the relationship between the individual and the universe was more mysterious, less certain, and most importantly – the stuff of poetry. Suddenly with Francis Bacon, Isaac Newton and the Royal Society the world became quite concrete, manageable and utterly explainable. Einstein, however, made it uncertain all over again; suddenly there were two observers on a train, and each of them had a different point of view.

Shakespeare, in his own way, set the precedent for Einstein and post-structuralism, for all of those who question our perceptions about the world. In this way he is frighteningly modern.

And this is also why Shakespeare's work is so relevant today.

Notes

[1]Frye, Northrop. "How True a Twain." *Northrop Frye's Writings on Shakespeare and the Re-naissance*. University of Toronto Press, 2010. 97

[2]Scaliger, *Poetices*. 1.i. 3(1)

[3]Foucault, M. *The History of Sexuality, Vol 1: An Introduction*. Knopf, Doubleday Publishing Group, 2012. 43

[4]Klawitter, George (ed.) *The Poems of Richard Barnfield*. iUniverse, Inc., 2005. 44

[5]Goldberg, Jonathon. *Sodometries*. Fordham University Press, 2010. 19

[6]Orgel, Stephen. "Nobody's Perfect: Or Why Did the English Stage Take Boys for Women?" *South Atlantic Quarterly* 88 (1989) 17

[7]Greenblatt, Stephen. *Renaissance. Self-fashioning from More to Shakespeare*. University of Chicago Press, 2005. 175

[8]Prynne, William. "Histriomastix: The Player's Scourge or Actor's Tragedy." *Early English Books Online*. ProQuest Information and Learning Company. Online. University of British Columbia. accessed 21 February 2007. 212

[9]Nelson, Alan. *Monstrous Adversary*. Liverpool University Press, 2003. 226

[10]Schiffer, James (ed.). *Shakespeare's Sonnets: Critical Essays*. Psychology Press, 2000. 21

[11]*Shakespeare's Sonnets*. Oxford University Press, 2003. 34

[12]*Hamlet*. (Folger, 2013.) 3.2 125-126

[13]*Twelfth Night*. (Folger,1993) 2.1 34-35

[14]Ibid., 2.1 36-38

[15]*The Merchant of Venice*. (Signet Classic, 1998) 2.8. 50.

[16]Ibid., 4.1. 281-285

[17]Fenton, James. *The Strength of Poetry*. Farrar, Straus and Giroux, 2002. 192.

[18]Kesson. A. *John Lyly and Early Modern Authorship*. Oxford University Press, 2014. 205

[19]Ibid., 5

[20]Ibid., 19

[21]Croll, Morris. "The Sources of Euphuistic Rhetoric." *Style, Rhetoric and Rhythm: Essays by Morris W. Croll*. Patrick, Max J. and Robert O. Evans (eds.) 241

[22]Taylor, Gary (ed). *The New Oxford Shakespeare: Complete Works*. Oxford University Press, 2016.1009 (footnote)

[23]*Romeo and Juliet*. (The RSC Shakespeare, 2009) 1.2. 38-41

[24]Carter, A. Daniel. *The Plays of John Lyly*. Bucknell University Press, 1988. 137

[25]*Hamlet*. (Folger, 1992) 3.2. 99-101

[26]*Twelfth Night*. (Folger 1993) 1.1. 1-4

[27]Carter, A. Daniel. *The Plays of John Lyly*. Bucknell University Press, 1988. 131

[28]*Hamlet*. (Folger, 1992) 3.1. 68-73

[29]Carter, A. Daniel. *The Plays of John Lyly*. Bucknell University Press, 1988. 113

[30]Ibid., 122-123

[31]Hunter, G.K. *John Lyly, The Humanist as Courtier*. Routledge and K, Paul, 1962. 31

[32]*Love's Labour's Lost*. (4.3) (Folger, 1996) 175.

[33]Ibid., (4.3) 222-225

[34]Ibid., (5.2) 285-288

[35]Ibid., (5.1) 133

[36]Ibid., (5.2) 947-948

[37]Legouis, Emile and Louis Camazian. *A History of English Literature, Vol. 1*. J.M. Dent and Sons, 1964. 271

[38]Ostermark-Johansen, Lena "The Death of Euphues: Euphuism and Decadence in Late Victorian Literature " *English Literature in Transition*, 1880-1920, Volume 45, Number 1, 2002. 5

[39]Ibid., 15

[40]Ibid., 18

[41]Ibid., 21

[42]Hunter, G.K. J*ohn Lyly, The Humanist as Courtier*. Routledge and K, Paul, 1962. 7

[43]Child, John Griffin. *John Lyly and Euphuism*. Erlangen and Leipzig, 1894. 9

[44]Hunter, G.K. John Lyly, *The Humanist as Courtier*. Routledge and K, Paul, 1962. 21

[45]Croll, Morris. "The Sources of Euphuistic Rhetoric " *Style, Rhetoric and Rhythm: Essays by Morris W. Croll*. Patrick, Max J. and Robert O. Evans (eds.) Princeton University Press, 1966. 269

[46]Ibid.

[47]Ostermark-Johansen, Lena. "The Death of Euphues: Euphuism and Decadence in Late Victorian Literature " *English Literature in Transition*, 1880-1920, Volume 45, Number 1, 2002. 5

[48]Ibid., 35

[49]Kesson. A.. *John Lyly and Early Modern Authorship*. Manchester University Press, 2014. 1

[50]Ibid., 1-2

[51]McNeely, Trevor. *Proteus Unmasked*. Lehigh University Press, 2004. 141

[52]Ibid., 125

[53]Ibid.

[54]Fryer, Jonathan. *Wilde*. Thistle Publishing, 2014. 105

[55]Oliver, Elizabeth. "Redecorating Vorticism: Marianne Moore's 'Ezra Pound' and the Geometric Style." *Journal of Modern Literature*, Vol. 3, No. 4. 85

[56]Ibid., 87

[57]Ibid.

[58]Ibid., 90

[59]Ibid., 92

[60]Cixous, Hélène. "The Laugh of the Medusa." *Signs*, Vol. 1, No. 4. 878

[61]De Beauvoir, Simone. *The Second Sex*. Vintage, 2011 837

[62]Ibid., 838

[63]Levin, Harry. "Observations on the Style of Ernest Hemingway." *The Kenyon Review*, Vol 13, No. 4. 584

[64]Kazin, Alfred. "Authors and Critics Appraise Works." *New York Times on the Web (Books)*. July 3, 1961. http://movies2.nytimes.com/books/99/07/04/specials/hemingway-obit4.html accessed April 10, 2019

[65]Levin, Harry. "Observations on the Style of Ernest Hemingway." *The Kenyon Review*, Vol 13, No. 4. 589

[66]Ibid., 605

CONCLUSION:

Beyond Science

"The word and the object are one."

Marshall McLuhan suggests that the ancient study of dialectics and the modern subject of science are predicated on the notion that the word and the object are the same thing. The ancient subject of grammar, on the other hand, is founded on a kind of scepticism/wonder about language that is characteristic of modern semiotics. McLuhan says that dialectics "insisted that all human language performed one and the same function in expressing the rational intentions of the human mind."[1] Grammar, in contrast "aimed to consider these problems which again today are in the forefront of linguistic study."[2] McLuhan would have certainly been aware of Ferdinand de Saussure. De Saussure – considered to be the founder of modern semiotics – theorized that there was no intrinsic relationship between the name of an object and the object itself. Language is therefore, arbitrary.

Shakespeare would agree with De Saussure that the word and the object are *not at all* the same thing. Language has its origins in the imagination, and truth is anything that the poet can persuade you is true. The polysemous nature of language guarantees that it is simultaneously untrustworthy and magical. Shakespeare believed – in the neoplatonic manner – that poetry (like all beauty) might give us a glimpse of God, or a glimpse of well – nothing. So how are we to tell which? Shakespeare's work warns us to be wary of the possibilities.

The dual nature of language is best exemplified by the concept of equivocation. In the 16th century most right-thinking

Englishmen believed Jesuits were traitorous Catholics who would do anything to destroy the Anglican church and murder Elizabeth. Several Jesuits were labelled "equivocators" because of their behaviour at their trials. Robert Southwell, who was hanged for treason in 1579, wrote a treatise on the subject of equivocation before he died. And Henry Garnet – executed in 1606 – was accused of having participated in the Gunpowder Plot. These equivocators claimed to be able to defend themselves by calling on the ancient Catholic belief that it was possible to say one thing to one's accuser while whispering the truth to God.

The Jesuit equivocator did not "lie." The fact that only God – not a human being – could hear the truth was not the fault of the equivocator; it was the fault of flawed human language. The Liar's Paradox (also called the Barber's Paradox) is relevant here: the liar who says: "I am lying." This highlights the difficulties of language. The existence of lying is a fundamental challenge to the holy relationship between words and things. And the Jesuits believed that the only being to whom we are obligated to tell the truth is God. The concept of equivocation is the theoretical equivalent of Shakespeare's attitude to poetry; a lie that tells the truth. All poetry, for Shakespeare, is simultaneously unreliable and deeply blessed.

Equivocation was articulated by the early modern philosopher Navarrus as proof of the general untrustworthiness of language. Navarrus (Martin de Azpilcueta,1491-1586) was a prominent 16th century philosopher and founder of the School of Salamanca. When Navarrus wrote about equivocation he stretched the definition beyond the spiritual and ethical issue of speaking a special truth to God. Navarrus hinted, in his writing on equivocation, at modern language theory.

Stefania Tutino says Navarrus theorized that "human language is not a tightly regulated venue where meaning is communicated between people, but a complex set of different types of communication, not a measure of moral uncertainty but a measure of hermeneutical uncertainty."[3] Navarrus went beyond the moral implications of equivocation to propose the radical idea that language itself is fundamentally equivocal. This makes all communication difficult and ambiguous. And that kind of scepticism about the relationship between signifier (word) and signified (object) is what characterizes modern day post-structuralist theory.

Frank Huntley tells us that in Shakespeare's lifetime Navarrus was well known to educated Europeans. He quotes from Etienne Pasquier's 1602 book *Jesuit Catechism*: "The great Canonist Navarre, the chiefest of all the Doctors in matters of the Canon-Law, speaking of this simple vow [i.e. equivocation] giues it the name of Great and Maruailous."[4] We have no proof that Shakespeare read Navarrus. However, if we understand the focus of *Macbeth* to be an expression of the fundamental mutability of language, then it is no accident that Shakespeare mentions equivocation again and again. That Shakespeare was obsessed with the ambiguous nature of language, that he found poetry both fair and foul, good and evil, attractive and unattractive – but always obsessively addictive – is proved by the many musings on language found in his work.

Shakespeare's attitude to language both predates and channels post-modern philosopher Ludwig Wittgenstein's theory of language games. McNeely suggests that in *King Lear* Shakespeare's many uses of the word "nature" "may illustrate the profundity of his awareness of Wittgenstein's law of the ultimate contextually of meaning."[5] In his theory of language games Wittgenstein uses the example of workers passing boxes. After awhile, the workers begin to use a kind of shorthand – instead of saying "please give me the box," they may say only "here." It is only in the context of "handing over something" that the word "here" actually comes to mean "give me the box." Wittgenstein concludes that different words mean different things in different contexts.

Post-structuralist Jacques Derrida's theory of "differance" says basically the same thing; that the meaning of any word is only clear in the syntactical context. Words do not have a discrete meaning. Derrida went even further though, in his obsession with language's ambiguities, when he went on to discuss the significance of what is known philosophically as the dilemma of the "law of the excluded middle." According to this Aristotelian principle, a thing cannot be itself and something else at the same time. That "excluded middle" is the possibility that in fact there is a third choice; an object can somehow be a combination of the two.

Shakespeare's use of the technique antanaclasis is ubiquitous and relevant to Wittgenstein's language games, and uses language to contradict the law of the excluded middle. Antanaclasis is a rhetorical term for punning; it is the kind of quibble so despised by Garrick and the members of the Royal Society. What makes antanaclasis a kind of "classier" pun is that the many meanings are not just funny, but typically express a paradoxical observation. Perhaps Shakespeare's most famous and challenging utilization of antanaclasis is in *Love's Labour's Lost*. In this passage Berowne questions the value of (what I would assume to be) Ramist scientific study: "As, painfully to pore upon a book / To seek the light of truth, while truth the while / Doth falsely blind the eyesight of his look. / Light, seeking light, doth light of light beguile" (1.1).

A down and dirty translation of the last line would be: "light" (the eye), by "seeking light" (seeking truth), "doth light of light beguile" (deprives the eye of vision).[6] In summary: If you imagine you're going to find "truth" in the dark recesses of books, pretty soon you'll be disappointed, because blindness will bar you from truth. The paradox here is that light may blind you. Shakespeare's bravado, his obvious joy – evident not only here but in many other passages, in many other plays – in celebrating the mutability of meaning, is clearly a kind of slap in the face to anyone who asserts that "the object and the word are one." And again – in Hermogenean fashion – the form of antanaclasis is related to the meaning. We needn't translate the many meanings of "light" in the passage to understand what it is being said about language; the repetition eloquently expresses hermeneutical uncertainty.

McNeely goes so far as to suggest that such a virtuoso linguistic performance tempts us to find a deeper, allegorical meaning – one which may elude us. He offers Shakespeare's definition of allegory, which is also Quintilian's, as "present[ing] with one thing in words or another in meaning or even something quite opposed."[7] McNeely believes that Shakespeare's message about language is the ultimate message of his rhetoric. On the surface Shakespeare seems to be critiquing language, but in reality he is also praising it; or in fact perhaps its the other way around. We are never quite sure what exactly he means. The point of Shakespeare's allegory, says McNeely is "that we can be fooled, that we can build a perfectly satisfactory reality on thin air and never think to question."[8]

This fooling, the 'pulling the wool over our eyes' is the ambiguous message Shakespeare wishes us to hear. But, is that all the greatest bard in English wishes to do? Inform us that language tricks us? How does he feel about that? And why is so important to critique language anyway?

This precise question is raised by philosophies that are lumped together lately under the category of 'theory' – by those who reject post-structuralism. Post-structuralists like Foucault, Barthes and Derrida try everyone's patience – not only because their writing is so dense – but because they are mainly concerned with parsing language and analyzing its effects on human perception. Does language really matter that much? Foucault thinks so, and his ideas on the subject are easier to understand by making reference to Oscar Wilde's essay *The Decay of Lying*.

Wilde's masterful philosophical tract sets the stage for post-structuralism much like Shakespeare did. *The Decay of Lying* is an impassioned and witty rant lamenting the decline of falsehoods. Wilde contends that facts – and here he is referring to the style of 'realism' that attempts to faithfully present reality – have ruined art. This is a classic Sophistic, anti-Stoic position. Wilde is suggesting that the poet's concern with truth has destroyed poetry. He suggests instead that the basis of all poetry is lies. Instead of advising poets to observe reality and report on it, he flips this concept around, suggesting art and poetry *create reality*. He illustrates his bizarre point with an equally bizarre analogy, announcing that: "At present, people see fogs, not because there are fogs, but because poets and painters have taught them the mysterious loveliness of such effects."[9]

But this outlandish statement makes more actual sense then you might think. He is not of course suggesting that, before Turner, Londoners were always – rain or shine – able to see their hands in front of their faces unobstructed by mist. He is merely suggesting that *the concept* of fog was not something that people thought about much before Turner. And then the artist – through his artificial representations of reality – made fog popular. Art and poetry create concepts. They do not merely effect the manner in which we see things, but they change our perceptions of reality.

Foucault claims that masturbation didn't exist until it was effectively 'discovered' by Tissot in 1760. Tissot's *L'Onanisme* blamed masturbation for a veritable litany of physical disorders. Again, Foucault is not suggesting that no one ever pleasured themselves before 1760. What he *is* suggesting is that people always touched themselves for pleasure, but it was considered inconsequential – not scandalous, not a 'thing.' And it was only when Tissot wrote about it, *in words*, that people formed the concept, and masturbation became what it is today; a habit which was once thought of as nasty, but that we now furiously try to convince ourselves is perfectly okay. Shakespeare's feats of legerdemain – in which he successfully pulls the wool over our eyes, while pointing to the virtuosity and flaws of his performance – open the door to the post-structuralist notion that language shapes our perceptions of the world. It is very important to analyze exactly how language does this and why.

Foucault and Shakespeare are twin figures. Both were dense stylists obsessed with the obfuscatory. Miller, Foucault's biographer and sometime psychoanalyst, suggests that Foucault – as a sado-masochistic homosexual with AIDS – found it best to hide his ideas and his personality in a complex, impenetrable style. Was Shakespeare also hiding something? Perhaps that he was a decadent bisexual nobleman named Edward de Vere – a poet who had squandered his fortune and died in disgrace? At any rate, for Miller, Foucault's rhetorical style is dangerous because it hides the author: "The dazzle and at times preciosity of the style combine with the minute dexterity of the analysis to produce obscurity in which both author and reader fade from view."[10]

This description of Foucault's style reads like a description of Shakespeare's as well. Foucault makes the shocking statement: "I am fully aware that I have never written anything other than fictions ... But I believe it is possible to make fictions function within truth."[11] Foucault seems to be suggesting that *all writing is fiction.*

From this it is a very short step to the notion that all *language* is fiction. This is what Shakespeare and post-structuralism wish us to understand. But does that mean we must reject language? No – for like democracy, it is unfortunately all we have. Are they suggesting then – like Ramus, the anti-theatricalists, and the Royal Society – that we should reject the double meanings, the playful ambivalences and allusions of poetry, as too dangerous?

No, Shakespeare and the modern post-structuralists are suggesting quite the opposite. Language deserves our deep respect and profound attention because, although we think it mirrors observed reality, it is often more akin to fantasy. Shakespeare, Wilde and Foucault are all quite intent on reminding us that often what we think is true is actually a lie, and that a lie can offer us truths that cannot be discovered through the scientific method.

McLuhan suggests that the principles behind Alfred Korzybski's pragmatic philosophy are akin to those of early modern grammar and modern structuralism. He says that among those modern philosophers who have followed in the neo-platonic, anti-Ramist school are "Count Korzybski and the Chicago University School of encyclopedists."[12] Korzybski is especially interesting, as his work offers a challenge to Aristotle, and a practical application of post-structuralist ideas.

'A is A' – Aristotle's law of identity – says that things are what we perceive them to be with our senses. Korzybski wrote *Science and Sanity: A Introduction to Non-Aristotelian Systems and General Semantics* in 1933. He says quite the opposite:

> If words are not things, or maps are not the actual territory, then obviously the only possible link between the objective world and the linguistic world is found in structure, and structure alone. The only usefulness of a map or a language depends on the similarity of structure between the empirical world and the map-languages. If the structure is not similar, then the traveller or speaker is led astray, which in serious human life-problems must become always eminently harmful.[13]

SHAKESPEARE BEYOND SCIENCE

For Korzybski, the 'structure' or language does not always accurately reflect the 'structure' of the world. Another way of saying that 'the map is not the territory' is to consider the 'multiordinal' nature of language ('m.o'):

> [T]he main characteristic of these multiordinal terms is found in that they have different meanings in general, depend on the order of abstractions. Without the level of abstraction being specified, a m.o term is only ambiguous; its use involves shifting meanings, variables and therefore … it may not be an exaggeration to say that the larger number of human tragedies, private, social, racial, are intimately connected [to this].[14]

Korzybski makes it clear that his non-Aristotelian system of epistemology is not logic; Korzybski rejects logic altogether. He believes that logic as we know it is related to our nervous system and not to any concrete observable reality, "involving some sort of internal orientations, or evaluations, which are not necessarily formalized. The analysis of such *living relations* is the sole object of general semantics as a natural *empirical science*."[15]

Korzybski asks us to challenge basic epistemological systems, and to replace the word 'the' with the word 'a.' For instance, if human beings spoke of 'a love I feel for you' as opposed to 'the love I feel for you' they might discuss what love actually means to different people, without harbouring the false assumption that everyone shares the same understanding of love. Korzybski believes that "no facts are free from 'doctrines': so whoever fancies he can free himself from 'doctrines' expressed in the structure of the language he uses [etc.] simply cherishes a delusion."[16]

There are dangers in trusting science too much, and a danger in pretending that science always has – and will always – remain untouched by emotion or intuition. Albert Einstein should not be held responsible for the atomic bomb, in the same way that Alan Turing should not be held responsible for the fact that your computer is a corporate spy. But we might think differently about the 'The Theory of Relativity' if it was known as 'A theory which makes it possible to engineer a blast so toxic that it can blow up the earth,' or if 'the computer' was called 'A convenient, very entertaining time-saving – yet paradoxically time-consuming – device, which appears to give you information but actually provides you with lots of entertaining opinions, and at the same time steals your data.'

The Milgram study (1963, Yale University) was one of the most famous scientific experiments of the 20th century. Unwitting participants were at first asked politely – and then finally summarily ordered – to give an electric shock to a person in the next room. They could not see the victim, but they could hear the person's cries. The inspiration for the experiment was the notion that, when Nazis killed and tortured their victims, many gave the excuse that they were 'just following orders.' Are most people capable of torturing a fellow human if they are ordered to do so? Are we by nature, obedient?

A majority of the participants were willing to inflict pain on the anonymous person in the next room. This led researchers to believe that most of us follow orders, no matter what the moral implications. But in recent years – after re-examining its findings, the conclusions of the Milgram Study were challenged. It's true that most people who participated in the experiment did obey. But the reason they complied was not because they were frightened or cowed, but because they wished to support what they thought was *a good cause*. And what was that cause?

The cause of science.

This should give us pause. Human history provides countless examples of how capable we are of committing the most vile and extreme acts in the name of religion. It seems quite possible that humans can be convinced to do much the same thing in the name of science. Do we need any more proof that science has become a kind of modern religion?

Just in case you think Korzybski – and his notion of rejecting 'A is A' – is unhinged, consider Thomas S. Kuhn. Kuhn is a contemporary scientist and philosopher who has dared to challenge the objectivity of traditional science, who suggests that the answers that scientists find are often related to their choice of questions. Kuhn's scepticism of science's relationship to reality is evident when he says: "Normal science, the activity in which most scientists inevitably spend almost all their time, is predicated on the assumption that the scientific community knows what the world is like."[17]

The basis of Kuhn's theory is the idea that scientific experimentation and logic are dedicated to preserving the paradigms discovered by the great scientists who dared to step out of the box and invent them, as "under normal conditions the research scientist is not an innovator but a solver of puzzles, and the puzzles upon which he concentrates are just those which he believes can be both stated and solved within the existing scientific tradition."[18] In other words, subjectivity is as valid to science as objectivity, because ultimately, when Einstein's ideas were competing with Newton's, there was – for a period – no objective reality. There were just two different conceptions of reality competing with each other. Then, finally, one paradigm won over the other, and scientists consequently began doing their research only in the context of the new paradigm.

Charles Biederman's *Art As The Evolution of Visual Knowledge* (1948) was dedicated to Korzybski. Biederman believed that art might be better than science at communicating the reality of the world. Here he is, quoted by Alistair Grieve, describing how to differentiate his theory from that of the creed of 19th century artists who painted pictures of trees and mountains:

> [T]he process from nature to the final object of art is this: we observe the rhythms of nature, study how which results in structural information; this is the structural Process level of nature, i.e., inferential abstractions about how nature builds. Now we do not directly transpose this information to our art, for this would result in mimetic activity rather the inventive intention of our art objective. We therefore TRANSLATE the process information into the terms of our MATERIAL AND OUR OBJECTIVE in much the same way as did the inventors of the airplane, their objective being the invention of a flying object but not the imitation of a bird.[19]

Biederman's notion of art is profoundly and deceptively intuitive rather than literally mimetic, and is redolent of Apollinaire's witty definition of surrealism: "When man resolved to imitate walking, he invented the wheel, which does not look like a leg. In doing this, he was practicing surrealism without knowing it."[20] In fact, one can see in Biederman and in surrealism perhaps a 20th century aesthetic to challenge the Vorticist masculinist school of Lewis, Pound and Hemingway. Like Shakespeare, Biederman and Apollinaire were not interested in reporting on reality, but in creating new realities that may shed more light on the world through fantasy.

It's unfortunate that fantasy and surrealism have been co-opted by the entertainment industry and we are now obsessed by comic book heroes who battle the end of the world. This is not what Biederman and Apollinaire are talking about when they suggest images that resemble vaguely – but are not exact imitations of – the world around us. And Hollywood's fantasies are not the same as medieval "phantasies." The medieval art of memory asked individuals to create strange, violent, sexual creatures for their own memory loci; nowadays we are fed a daily supply of other people's strange, violent, sexual images, many of which we now have seen so many times that they are not very startling at all. And these modern "fantastical" narratives are uniformly banal: Even when the movie features "Transformers," the boy always gets the girl, and the virtuous and well-intentioned hero always wins the war against the evil forces of the universe. There are outliers – that is profound writers of science fiction (Samuel Delaney comes to mind) – but they tend not to be "popular."

Adorno was a Marxist philosopher and early member of the Frankfurt School who, like Wilde, celebrated art that does *not* reflect our daily reality and has *no* redeeming moral purpose. His theory about the modern film industry, expressed in *The Culture Industry: Enlightenment as Mass Deception*, is that the content of modern commercial films is not their forgettable narratives, but (wait for it!) money. Speaking of the filthy rich who run Hollywood, Adorno says: "There is at least the agreement – or at least the determination – of all executive authorities not to produce or sanction anything that in any way differs from their own rules, their own ideas about consumers, or above all themselves,"[21] and "the triumph of invested capital, whose title as absolute master. is etched deep into the hearts of the dispossessed in the employment line; it is the meaningful content of every film, whatever plot the production team may have selected."[22]

I would add that in commercial fantasy films today the content is definitely money – but sometimes that capital is expressed in the form of technology. We go to films to marvel at Marvel Comics and say to ourselves: 'Look at what all that money can do!' Fantasy films are, paradoxically, a celebration of the achievements of science.

Adorno – though a Marxist – rejects the didacticism of Brecht – (here quoted by Jodi Dean) "Whatever is educational in Brecht's plays can be taught more convincingly by theory – if it needs teaching at all."[23] His argument is precisely the opposite of Sidney's Ramistic argument in *In Defence of Poetry*. Adorno (quoted here by Ronald Bush) says art must "elevate social criticism to the level of form, de-emphasizing manifestly social content accordingly."[24]

The medium is the message; we are back to McLuhan, Shakespeare, and Hermogenes. Adorno believes that art presents us with images that are not exactly like life, but resemble it, and by making the comparison between those fantasies and our own real life we learn, think, meditate – and are alternately disturbed, or ecstatic.

What does it actually mean to discover a truth through art, without using the scientific method, contradicting the notion that one thing *cannot* be something else, and suggesting instead that a word is *not* necessarily equivalent to an object? Any of the countless paradoxical metaphors utilized by Shakespeare offer examples. Paul Strathern, writing about Derrida, uses Shakespeare as an example of Derrida's linguistic theory and the excluded middle. He considers: "All the world's a stage and all the men and women merely players." According to Aristotle's law of the excluded middle the world is a place where we really exist, and actors on a stage are merely acting out a fantasy. These are two different things, and they can never be the same. But metaphor allows us to see a deeper truth than the scientific method – that life can be real and "a play" at the same time. We certainly need our technologies and we need the scientific method for the practicalities of day to day life. But, though Art and poetry might not offer seamless answers to every day questions, they can shed light on perhaps what is a deeper reality.

Jacob Bronowski in *Science and Human Values* suggests we examine Leonardo Da Vinci's *Lady with an Ermine*, painted approximately 60 years before Shakespeare was born. The lady is lovely; the ermine, in its own way, is lovely. Keep looking at the painting – the lady begins to look an awful lot like the ermine. There is something unreal about both the ermine and the lady, as the lady is so ermine-like, and the ermine so ladylike. Bronowski suggests that this painting channels Darwin's theory of evolution, approximately 220 years before Darwin was born.

I submit that this painting is the visual equivalent of Shakespeare's rhetoric. Puttenham in his *Art of English Poesie* often compares poetry to painting. Shakespeare merely says: "Look at this, look at that." And inevitably, *this* is very like – or very unlike – *that*. Perhaps the Lady and the Ermine are not discrete and separate beings, separated by the names which categorize them via Aristotelian epistemological practices – perhaps they are *the same*.

When we write and/or speak, when we read creative writing or listen to a persuasive speech, we think about it all, and ask some questions, feel a shiver of pleasure. The author has expressed it, they have put it into words. Putting something into words is sometimes the equivalent of thinking, a metaphor is a kind of thought; it is thinking through comparison.

I feel this as I am writing this now. I do not know particularly how it will end up, but I know it will finish soon. Writing this, forming words, forming sentences, is a certain type of learning, a certain kind of creation, and yes, discovery.

I just need to mention that they are gradually killing humanities departments in universities in North America, and – much like the days when Ramus' teachings were ruling post-secondary institutions across Europe – pragmatic students are starting to demand, not poetry, but *useful* knowledge. I also think of a quote I heard somewhere recently – you know, one of those bits of "information" you read on the web – "In 2020 people will talk more to their automated response system than to their partners."

A fantasy maybe. But is it true? Maybe. What happens when we – to paraphrase the early modern rhetoricist Ascham – "care not at all for the manner of speaking, but only for 'the facts'"?

Conversely, what happens when you think about something, and then turn to someone, say it out loud, put that thought into words? It becomes something real, living, *persuasive*. Your thoughts have come alive for a moment; it's a little bit frightening – the words have a life of their own. And you don't know quite what that *being* you have created is. But you *like* the words, at least you think you do. *Well, I dare you to believe those words are true.*

Notes

1McLuhan, Marshall. *The Classical Trivium*. Gingko Press, 2006. 182
2Ibid.
3Tutunio, Sefania, *Shadows of Doubt: Language and Truth in Post-Reformation Catholic Culture*. London, 2014. 24
4Huntley, Frank L., *Macbeth and the Background of Jesuitical Equivocation*, PMLA. Vol. 79, No. 4, 396
5McNeely, Trevor. *Proteus Unmasked*. Lehigh University Press, 2004. 247
6*Love's Labour's Lost*. (Folger, 1996) 1.1. 76-79
7McNeely, Trevor. *Proteus Unmasked*. Lehigh University Press, 2004. 111
8Ibid., 121
9Wilde, Oscar, *Intentions*. Prometheus Books, 2004. 37
10Miller, James, *The Passion of Michel Foucault*, (Harvard University Press, 1993), 153
11Blanchot, Maurice *Foucault Blanchot*, (Zone Books, 1987) 94
12McLuhan, Marshall. *The Classical Trivium*. Gingko Press, 2006. 27
13Korzybski, Alfred. *Science and Sanity*. Institute of GS, 1958. 61
14Ibid., 74
15Ibid., xxix
16Ibid., 87
17Kuhn, Thomas. *The Structure of Scientific Revolutions*. University of Chicago Press, 1970. 5
18Kuhn Thomas. "Scientific Revolutions." *The Philosophy of Science*. Boyd, Richard and Philip Gaspar (eds.). MIT,1991. 144
19Grieve, Alastair. "Charles Biederman and the English Constructionists I: Biederman and Victor Pasmore" *The Burlington Magazine* 124, 954, 1982. 541
20Apollinaire Guillaume. "The Mammaries of Tiresias." *Three Pre-Surrealist Plays*. Slater, Maya (trans.). Oxford University Press, 1997 153-154.
21Adorno, Theodor, and Max Horkheimer. "The Culture Industry: Enlightenment as Mass Deception." *Production of Cultures, Cultures of Production*. du Gay, Paul (ed). Open Univeristy, 1997. 106
22Ibid., 107
23Dean, Jodie. *Cultural Studies and Political Theory*. Cornell University Press, 2000. 144
24Bush, Ronald. "Quiet, Not Scornful?" *A Poem Containing History: Textual Studies in The Cantos*. Lawrence Rainey S. (ed.) University of Michigan Press, 1997. 20

A Note on the Cover Image: Hilliard's miniature:
Man Grasping a Hand from a Cloud
(featuring the mysterious motto 'Attici, Amoris Ergo')

Morris Croll tells us that for rhetors in the early modern period the word 'Attic' commonly referred to Greek rhetoric, specifically what was called the 'anti-Ciceronian' style. The rhetorical controversy was principally over the relationship between the three styles articulated by Cicero: the humble, the medium and the grand. Cicero believed that the styles should be separate, but that each had its proper place. The anti-Ciceronians also believed that the three styles should be separate, but only approved of the humble style. Demosthenes' revolutionary notion opposed the separation of rhetorical styles. His speeches placed humble, medium, and grand sentences side by side. Demosthenes was the idol of the Greek rhetorician Hermogenes. *Shakespeare Beyond Science* proposes that Hermogenes also became – through Edward de Vere's apprenticeship with Johannes Sturm – *Shakespeare's* rhetorical model. Through his association with Hermogenes' radical rhetorical technique, Shakespeare would be seen in the early modern period, as an 'attic' poet, and 'anti-Ciceronian.' Thus the motto on Hilliard's miniature portrait 'Attici amoris ergo' can be translated as: 'Hermogenean rhetoric (Attici) results in (ergo; therefore) love (amoris).' (Love is a neo-platonic synonym for beauty.) Leslie Hotson suggests that Hilliard's miniature portrait is indeed a portrait of Shakespeare. The red-headed young man wears a hat – an iconographic representation of the Greek God Mercury – who in early modern times was associated with the kind of poetry that speaks directly to *all people.* Thus the portrait tells us that Shakespeare – through his mastery of the accessible, radical, eclectic style of Hermogenes – was able to communicate truth (the hand of God reaching from a cloud).

Acknowledgements

Michael Kositsky, Sally Clark, Ian Jarvis, and The Shakespeare Oxford Fellowship.

About the Author

Sky Gilbert is a poet, novelist, actor, playwright, filmmaker, theatre director, and drag queen extraordinaire. He believes that "poetry must be free." He has been a ground-breaking activist and a controversial personality in the Canadian theatre community – and the Canadian queer community – for nearly 40 years. He has had more than 40 plays produced, and written 7 critically acclaimed novels including *Guilty* (also translated into French), *Brother Dumb*, *Wit in Love*, and *Come Back* and three award winning poetry collections – *Digressions of A Naked Party Girl*, *Confessions of a Juvenile Delinquent* and *A Nice Place to Visit*, as well as a memoir, *Ejaculations from the Charm Factory*. His plays, including the iconic *Drag Queens on Trial*, have found a place in the Canadian theatrical canon. He has received three Dora Mavor Moore Awards for his theatre work, as well as the Pauline McGibbon Award, and The Silver Ticket Award. He also received the ReLit Award for his novel *An English Gentleman* in 2004. There is a street in Toronto named after him: "Sky Gilbert Lane." Dr. Sky Gilbert is a Professor at the School of English and Theatre Studies in Guelph where he specializes in creative writing, theatre and sexuality, and Shakespeare.